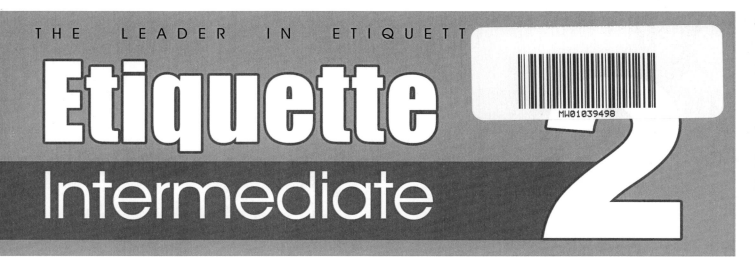

THE LEADER IN ETIQUETT

Etiquette
Intermediate

2

For ages 4th grade and up.

This Program Includes:

- ✿ 125 Etiquette Lessons
- ✿ Daily Activity Suggestions
- ✿ Fun, Easy Reading

The Leader in Etiquette Education

www.TheEtiquetteFactory.com

by Monica Irvine

© 2010
Etiquette Factory Publishing
ISBN # 978-0-9845046-1-9

862 Hansmore Place
Knoxville, TN 37919

www.TheEtiquetteFactory.com

Other books by this author include:
Etiquette for Beginners
Etiquette Masters

Table of Contents

Introduction

Hello and welcome to The Etiquette Factory—the 5th Core. You have made a wise decision that can literally change your children's future. Proper etiquette is something that is necessary to ensure a successful life both personally and professionally, but it is also the "key" to a happy, peaceful life. Don't worry, we will take it slow. This curriculum is designed with a very simple, yet efficient approach. Daily discussion with a parent or teacher is instrumental in the success of this program. You and your children will enjoy and even look forward to the few minutes you take each day to learn and practice these etiquette skills.

How Does This Program Work?

1. Each day, you and your student will separately or together, read the lesson. The lessons are written directly to the students and take about 5 minutes to read.

2. After reading, simply discuss what you've read. Allow your children to ask questions, ponder, and discuss that particular etiquette skill.

3. After most lessons, there is a suggested activity to reinforce the etiquette skill. I can't express enough what a difference participating in these activities can make, especially the role playing activities.

That's it; simple, efficient and really productive. You are going to be amazed at the progress your children make in etiquette and social graces as they work through this program.

If you really want these etiquette skills to become a part of your children's lives, may I make these suggestions?

- Parents (teachers), practice what you preach.
- Invite the whole family to participate in the etiquette training.
- The first year, simply go through the curriculum as instructed. A second year, go through the manual again, but this time, have your child (children) actually teach the etiquette skills. If you have more than one child, allow them to take turns teaching. Teaching these skills is a great way to remember them.
- Don't become the "etiquette police", just the etiquette example. We don't want our children to "cringe" when they hear the word etiquette. Compliment your children often, as you witness them practicing their etiquette skills. Look for gentle ways to discuss areas in need of improvement. Be positive. Have fun, and Love Those Children!

Day 1
What is Etiquette?

Hello and welcome to Etiquette in Training. I hope you are as excited as I am about learning skills that will positively affect your future, both personally and professionally. What does that mean? Well, it means that when you learn and use proper etiquette, people are drawn to you. That can help in many ways, including helping you to have more friends who admire great qualities in a person, helping you to have better relationships with your family, friends, teachers, etc., and, one day, helping you secure the job of your dreams, and much, much more. Actually, learning etiquette can be quite fun and exciting, because each day you are going to learn a skill. I like to think of these skills as "tools", which can be used to build your "house" (your life).

I know that you are familiar with builders. I hope that you, like me, have studied architecture during your history studies. Isn't it fascinating to see what people have built and designed since the beginning of time? Well, architecture, as you know, is greatly affected by the kinds of tools builders and designers have available to them. Think about it. You couldn't build a castle if all you had was a hammer. You would need tools that cut through stone, and you would need skilled professionals who know how to melt and shape iron and other metals. You would need engineers who could tell you how tall to build your castle. As you can see, you would need many different tools and skills that would all work together to build your great masterpiece.

Well, guess what? You are going to build something much more important than a castle; you are going to build your life, a great masterpiece. I know this project is very important to you. It's important to me, too. I want to help you build this important masterpiece. In order to do that, you need to collect as many tools as you can. You need to learn how to use these tools, know when to use them and why. Now, I don't have all the tools you'll need to build your life. You'll get tools from many people, such as your parents, teachers and mentors. You'll also get tools from books, and from experiences throughout your life, that will help you build your masterpiece. Get all you can. Surely, you can see that the more tools you possess and the more skills you acquire, the greater your masterpiece will be. Enjoy the journey.

So what is Etiquette? ***Etiquette is a set of guidelines for behavior that contributes positively to a society.*** Basically, it's rules that we try to follow that help others as well as ourselves to feel better. The goal of proper etiquette is to help make those around us feel comfortable and valued. The fun thing about that is that when we concentrate on making others feel comfortable, we end up with the biggest present of all—self-respect. Come with me while we learn etiquette rules, and when we're finished with this manual, I'll ask you if you know what self-respect means. I hope you'll be able to tell me. See you next time!

Day 2
Integrity

Do you know what integrity is?

Integrity is following a moral code of conduct. A moral code is basically a set of rules of appropriate or "right" behavior. Now, you may be thinking that not everyone shares the same rules of appropriate behavior, but usually in a society there are certain rules of behavior that are viewed as wrong or right. For instance, I think we can all agree that stealing is wrong. An example of moral behavior would be when we see someone fall down and hurt themselves; we would go and try to help that person. When we have integrity, it means we try to do what is right. Sometimes people may disagree on what is right and wrong, but as long as we try to live by our moral code of conduct, then we will demonstrate integrity. Integrity is a great quality to have, because it means that we do what we say we will do. It also means that we act according to how we believe. Wouldn't it be great if everyone in the world did what they promised, or behaved in the way they knew was right? This week, I want us to try to improve our integrity. We can do this by keeping our word. When we tell someone we're going to do something, let's do it. When others are counting on us to perform a task, let's complete it on time and properly. Take notice of how our feelings about ourselves will improve. It's a great feeling. Try it. See you next time.

Activity
Take a couple of minutes to discuss commitments that everyone in the family or group can make this week. They can be as simple as helping Mom wash the dishes, making our beds or teaching a younger sibling to ride their bike. Whatever it is, write down everyone's commitment for the week and then in one week, check to see if everyone kept their commitment. Sing praises for successes and remind everyone that keeping our commitments is a great example of integrity.

Day 3
Saying "Hello"

What happens when we say hello to someone?

Well, a couple of things actually. Number one, we stop "our life" for just a moment to take the time to say to another person through a little word (hello, hi), that our life is not too busy, not too "crazy", that we can't take a moment to recognize him/her. That's all it takes, just a moment. But in that moment, we relay a very important message: a message that tells another, **"You are important and I see you."** Simple, right? Number two; when we begin a conversation with a greeting like "Hello", we're actually sending "well wishes" to the person we are talking to. The definition of "greeting" is well wishes. That means that with the little words "hello, hi, good morning," etc., we are actually saying, "I'm so glad to see you. I hope you're having a marvelous day and I hope that all is well and good in your life. I care about you and wish you the very best." Wow!!!! I bet you didn't know you were saying all that with the little word hello, but you are. Beginning a conversation or a meeting with others with an appropriate greeting helps put others at ease and encourages feelings of kindness and compassion for one another. That's awesome. This week, try really hard to take the time to say hello to people when they enter a room, or pass you in the hall or anytime you see someone for the first time in your day. It's so much fun, really! See you next time.

Activity

It's time to do some research. See if you can translate the word "hello" into ten different languages. This is so helpful when you meet people from different countries. Greeting people in their "home" language is a great way to help them feel comfortable.

Hola   Nǐ hǎo

Bonjour   li-hó

Privet   Hallå

Hallo   Xin chào

Ciao

Kon'nichiwa

Day 4
Stand Up

Did you know that another way to show others polite respect is to stand when we greet each other? There are many good times to greet someone, like when walking into class in the mornings and seeing your teacher for the first time that day, or when grandparents or other adults enter a room. It is very respectful to stand and say hello. The standing sends a message to the one we are greeting that we honor them and respect who they are. Have you ever seen soldiers stand at attention when their superior officer walks into the room? It's amazing the feelings of gratitude that standing for someone else brings. Next time Grandma or any other adult stops by your home, try this experiment and see what happens. When the adult walks into the room, stop playing your video game or whatever you're playing or watching, stand and walk over to them and say, "Hi Grandma. I'm so glad you're here. Come sit by me." What feelings of love and appreciation Grandma or anyone else would have with such a welcome. I've found that the best way to help us learn this skill is to role play. Role play the "right way" to greet someone and have some laughs as you role play the "wrong way". Play both the Grandma, Dad, teacher, etc. and then play the child. This actually can be a lot of fun especially when you come up with different situations. Just remember, learning proper etiquette is important, but if we're going to remember a new skill, we must practice it. See you next time.

Day 5
Introductions

Another important part of greetings are introductions (telling or being told someone's name). Why is it important to learn each other's names? Well, have you ever met someone and then maybe a week later, you run into them at the park and they come up and say, "Hi, Zach. It's nice to see you again."? If you're Zach, you're probably thinking, "Wow, he remembered my name. He knows who I am." But if you're Zach and he comes up to you and says, "Hi, Theodore. It's nice to see you again," you're probably thinking, "Wow, he doesn't have a clue who I am." When others call us by name, it makes us feel more important. It makes us feel good that they remember who we are. That's why it is so important to try really hard to remember others' names. Remember, etiquette is helping others feel comfortable and valued. Here are some hints to help you remember others' names when you are being introduced:

1. Repeat their name several times in your mind.

2. Think of something to connect their name with. For instance; if you're introduced to Jordan, think of the river Jordan. If you're introduced to Sam, think of Uncle Sam. If you're introduced to Luke, think of Luke Skywalker from Star Wars. You can't always think of something, but you will be surprised how many connections you can make between names and other familiar thoughts.

3. Use their name quickly, for example saying, "Oh Summer, it's so nice to meet you."

4. When you're being introduced to someone, be quiet, listen carefully and repeat their name to make sure you heard it right. For instance, say, "Did you say Mr. Jones? Well, it's so nice to meet you Mr. Jones."

Activity
Practice remembering names this week. The "hints" you come up with are private and for your benefit only; however a word of warning: make sure when you come up with a "hint" to help you remember someone's name, it is respectful and does not "make fun" in any way of that person. Good luck and I'll see you next time.

Day 6
More Introduction Etiquette

Here are a few more tips I wanted to give you concerning introductions. Did you know that it's your job to introduce people who don't know each other? For example, let's say you and your best friend Taylor walk into a movie theater where you see some of your friends from church, who Taylor doesn't know. After you say "hello" (or greet) your friends, introduce Taylor to everyone. This helps Taylor to feel included.

If you happen to go into a room by yourself and you don't know the other people in the room, be BRAVE… introduce yourself. I know this seems like a very scary thing to expect you to do, but you would be surprised how much better everyone in the room will feel when everyone has been introduced. You have to decide if you are going to be the brave one or not.

Finally, what if a person makes a mistake in saying your name? Proper etiquette says, "Don't correct people in public." You don't ever want to embarrass someone or make them feel bad that they said the wrong name, so instead of saying anything immediately, wait until you can take that person aside and say something like, "I know you didn't mean to, but you called me Sparky and my name is Zeek." Now you've spared their feelings and that's a really good thing. OK, it's time to role play. Get up and practice. See you next time.

Activity
This is a great skill to "role play". Let the kids take turns introducing each other and even introducing themselves. To get some laughs, see who can come up with the most unique name and whoever laughs first, looses. Keeping a straight face is the key. Have Fun!

Day 7
Addressing "Grown-Ups"

What should we call grown-ups?
Well, it's polite to use Mr. and Mrs. unless told otherwise. Titles are given to adults to show signs of respect and sometimes to acknowledge acts of accomplishment. For instance, we say Mr. or Sir to express our respect for an older man. We sometimes say Mrs. (if married) or Ms. (if unmarried) to show respect to an older woman. When someone receives his/her doctorate degree, we call him/her Doctor (Dr.) and then their last name. Titles are also given to family members to show love and affection. For instance, we say Aunt Mary or Uncle Bill or Grandma Madewell or Grandpa Hill. These titles let those around us know that they are our family and we are proud to announce to the world our relationship with them. They also make our family members feel important and loved.

When is it OK to call an adult by their first name? Well, families might have different rules when it comes to this, so be sure and check with your family concerning family traditions and such. Usually, it is not OK to call an adult by their first name unless they have asked or invited you to. Even though an adult has asked you to call them by their first name, may I suggest that you still clear it with your parents. Don't worry, if it sounds a little complicated, but I bet you're already doing these things. See you next time.

Activity
Discuss with your parents regarding the adults in your life who you do not refer to as Mr. or Mrs. Make sure Mom and Dad are both comfortable with these decisions. Sometimes, it is appropriate to call an adult by their first name with a Mr. or Mrs. in front of it, for example: Mr. Charles or Mrs. Kathy. This is less formal but still shows respect for their age.

Day 8
When to Shake Hands

Gentlemen (all males young and old) always extend their hand when greeting another gentleman. It is simply the polite thing to do. You don't have to wait until you're a grown-up to perform this act of good manners; start today.

When a gentleman greets a lady (all females young and old), he should wait to see if the lady extends her hand. If she does, then the gentleman takes it. If the lady does not extend her hand, then the gentleman simply nods his head.

If a gentleman extends his hand when greeting a lady, it is polite for the lady to take his hand.

Shaking hands is a warm way to say hello. Your handshake should be firm, but not too hard as it would be uncomfortable to the one shaking your hand. Too weak of a handshake, might send a message of indifference (a lack of concern or interest), so work on the perfect handshake.

Activity
Definitely, let's get up and practice. Remember the rules. Try to see if you can trick each other into shaking when you're not suppose to and not shake when you should. You need males and females to practice the rules thoroughly. It will be lots of fun. See you next time.

Day 9
"Magic Words"

Please, Thank You and You're Welcome:

I bet you didn't know these words were "magic" but guess what. They are! Why magic? Well, do you think it's magic when you ask for something and it just appears? I do. I love it when that happens. I have discovered that there are three words that somehow make my life SO MUCH EASIER!!!! Sometimes we don't want to use these words because we're tired or mad or don't feel like we should have to say them. I have felt like that before. But we should remember that using the words please, thank you, and you're welcome actually helps us more than it does anyone else. Hopefully though, we want to use these words also because they show gratitude for others for sharing or taking the time to help us in some way. For instance, let's say you walk into your sister's room and say, "Mary, would you please help me with my homework? I'm kind of stuck on a problem." Then after Mary has graciously helped you, you say; "Thank you so much Mary for taking the time to help me. I really appreciate it." It may seem like it would be hard, but, really, it is so simple. By using these words, you sent a polite message to Mary that said you appreciate her and you know her time is valuable. If you tried it without those words, you're likely to still be working on that math problem. Try it….I dare ya! See you next time.

Activity
For one day, keep a chart of how many times you used the words thank you, please and you're welcome. As a family, share your charts with each other.

Day 10
Making Mistakes

Let's discuss making mistakes. What did we say was proper etiquette when someone mispronounced our name? Right, we don't correct in public. Well, we all "goof up" sometimes, even us adults. It's not always fun to make a mistake, but our disappointment or embarrassment can be lessened, depending on how those around us react to our mistake. For instance, let's say you're walking down the hall at school and you trip and fall. All of a sudden, you're on the floor and you're really embarrassed. You feel kind of clumsy. What if someone bent down and started to help you pick up your things and said, "Oh if you think this is bad, you should have seen me do a complete "360" into a puddle of mud last week. It was Ug......ly!" You would probably laugh and then not feel like you were the only "clumsy one" in school. What that person did in this situation was the definition of etiquette—making others feel comfortable. Whenever you can, take the opportunity to help someone by not drawing attention to their mistakes. Let's make sure we are never guilty of laughing at others' mistakes (unless they are laughing too) or pointing out others' mistakes to other people. This is not proper etiquette. The best advice I can give you when you make a mistake, is to quickly say you're sorry if it involves another person and if the only person it involves is you—laugh. It's the best medicine. Hopefully we will learn from our mistakes and then move on. See you next time.

Activity
Everyone share an incident when you have made a mistake. Talk about how those around you reacted and how their reactions made you feel. Discuss ways that those reactions might have been handled with etiquette in mind.

Day 11
"Blaming Others"

I want to talk to you about one other aspect of making mistakes; blaming others for our mistakes or blaming others when an incident was simply an accident. I know that probably none of us likes to think that we are ever guilty of this, but I have found that it is easier than we think to blame others. For instance, imagine you are out on the playground playing tag with your friends. You're running and having a great time when all of a sudden someone else runs right into you. What do you do? I want you to ask yourself what your typical reaction would be in this type of situation. Would you immediately say, "Hey, you should have been watching where you were going!"? Or would you have been more likely to say, "Are you O.K.?" In situations like these, we must realize that, more than likely, the person who ran into us did not do it on purpose. It was an accident. Regardless if it was a careless accident (the person should have been paying better attention), it still was an accident. Remember our etiquette rule is to help others feel at ease and comfortable. Let me give you an example of a possible response to this situation with proper etiquette in mind: "Oh goodness, are you OK? I'm sorry, I should be more careful when I'm running." Now wait, I know what you're thinking. You're thinking, "Why am I the one apologizing? It wasn't my fault." Well, you're right. But you would be amazed at the message you send, when you take some of the responsibility of such an incident. It tells someone that you're not above making a mistake and you're not so quick to accuse others of wrongdoing. You will be respected for your willingness to apologize. The same goes for taking responsibility when you do make a mistake. Some of us tend to blame others or blame situations for our mistakes. Remember, the strongest, bravest, most admirable people are those who take responsibility for their own actions. Can you imagine your dad walking into the room and hearing you and your sibling arguing and he says, "OK, enough of this. Now I want to know who started this argument?" And you answer, "I did". Would your dad fall over in shock or what? I know that regardless of the punishment, you would gain the trust and respect of your father. Give it some thought. I'll see you next time.

Activity
Discuss this topic as a family or class.

Day 12
Tact

What is tact?

Tact is the ability to deal with others without offending them. So as we improve our ability to be more "tactful" in different situations, we will enjoy our relationships with others more fully. Now let me make something very clear: tact is not lying. It is not being deceitful in any way. It is simply the ability to see the positive in situations, in people, instead of focusing on the negative. Let me give you an example. Let's say your mom makes dinner and is excited for her family to try a new casserole dish. Everyone sits down at the dinner table and proceeds to try the casserole, but it's terrible. What do you do? What do you say? You don't want to hurt mom's feelings. She obviously is trying hard to find new things that her family will like. It takes time to go to the grocery store, buy the food, come home and prepare it, clean up the kitchen and then hope that everyone enjoys this new dish. Being tactful in this situation is to come up with something you can say to make your mom know how much you appreciate the effort she has put into this dinner, regardless of how you feel about the casserole. A suggestion might be, "Wow Mom, you really went to a lot of trouble to make this a special meal. I appreciate all you do for our family and for always trying to find new things we will like." Now do you think Mom will really care if you don't like the casserole? I doubt it. She will feel appreciated and loved and that's what she really wants. Try it. I'll see you next time.

Activity

Give directions to the class that they have 5 minutes to draw a portrait of themselves using crayons. 5 minutes only. Then, one at a time, allow the kids to come up front and show their portrait to the rest of the class. Instruct the class that their job is to find things that they can compliment the artist on and give their compliments. What do they like about the photo? Only positive remarks are allowed. This is tact, not lying but looking for the positive.

Day 13
Rudeness

Have you ever been rude?
Well, have you ever sneezed without covering your nose or burped with your mouth open without saying "excuse me"? If you are guilty of either of those kinds of things, you have been rude. I know most of the time we don't mean to be rude, but sometimes our body acts more quickly than we can control. If that ever happens, the thing to do is to quickly apologize and take responsibility for your actions. It is important to realize that the way we act affects those around us. When we are rude, it can make those around us unhappy and uncomfortable. Be sensitive to those around you.

Now what if someone is rude to you? I know it's probably easier to just get mad and be rude in return when someone has been rude to us, but that is not proper etiquette. The #1 best way to combat rudeness is with kindness. I'm serious. It works (well, most of the time). Let's say you're playing basketball in the gym and you need a drink of water, so you leave for a minute to get a drink. Upon your return, there is someone else with the basketball. You walk up to that person and say, "Hey, I was playing with that ball before I went to get a drink. Could I have it back?" The person says, "Too bad for you," and continues to play with the ball. What do you do? I know what you would like to do, but let's talk about what you should do. May I suggest a response with etiquette in mind: "Oh well, I'm glad you came into the gym. I wanted someone to play with. It's always more fun with two. Would you like to play a game?" Even if that person declines the request, you have done your best to improve the situation and you should be proud of yourself. I know I would be proud of you. See you next time.

Activity
This is an important topic that can use a lot of discussion. Help your class come up with many examples of rude behavior and how they could use kindness to defuse the situation. Let them get up and practice. Set up scenes of rude behavior and then let your students react to the situations the best way they can with etiquette in mind. This really helps prepare them for facing these situations in their life. Practice, practice, practice.

Day 14
Giving and Receiving Apologies

We've already discussed briefly giving apologies, but did you know that there are two parts to apologies. Well, there are. The first part is making sure our apologies sound sincere. That means being honest about the apology. Usually people can tell if someone is really sorry or not. For instance, has your sibling ever done something to you and your mom sees it and then makes your sibling apologize to you. You get a very insincere "Soorrrry" or maybe you get a real short and abrupt "Sorry", but you can tell they don't really mean it. Remember as we increase our integrity, we have to make sure we're honest in all things; that includes our apologies.

The second step in a successful apology, is accepting the apology graciously (that means compassionately and mercifully). Basically, when we receive a sincere apology, our etiquette behavior must "kick in"; which means now our job is to help make others feel comfortable and valued. So how do we do that after an apology? May I suggest something like this; "Oh that's OK. You didn't mean to splash me. Let's go jump off the diving board." The point is, accept the apology and then move on. Sometimes, we like to keep bringing up an occasion when someone has upset us in some way, but if we have received a sincere apology, then it is polite to not bring up past offenses. It's a great way to live. Try it! I'll see you next time.

Activity
This is a great subject to "role play". Allow your children to set up scenes where an accident has taken place. Practice apologizing and accepting the apology graciously; for instance, have one child walk away from his seat and another child take it. Analyze how everyone handled it and look for ways to improve. Have some laughs, its fun.

Day 15
Accepting the Word "NO"

If you're like me, there are times when you really don't like to hear the word no. Sometimes when you're a kid, it seems you get told no more than any other word. All I can say to comfort you is that one day, you'll hopefully be a parent and then you can "dish out" as many no's as you like. Until then, however, I think we need to figure out how to handle this word with a little more grace. Basically, that means we can't sprawl out on the floor with our heads, hands and feet pounding uncontrollably until our clothes are drenched in sweat, just because we were told we can't have cookies and milk for breakfast. This would not be considered proper etiquette. A polite way to respond would be something like, "OK, thanks

"I Said No!"

for thinking about it Mom. I guess I'll just eat "Cookie Crunch" with milk instead." It is rude to continue to ask for something after you have been told "No" or to whine, cry, scream, sulk or pout. These types of behaviors are definitely not attractive and show signs of poor self control. You know, it's easy to have manners when everything is going our way, but the real test of our integrity is when things don't go our way. That's when we really show our self respect. I know it's not easy but with practice, we can all be better at accepting the word no in a way we can be proud of. See you next time.

Activity
Share an experience you've had with your family when something didn't go your way. Explain why you were disappointed in the situation and how you handled it. Ponder whether there could have been other ways to handle your disappointment.

Day 16
When is it OK for You to Say "No"?

Yes, oh how we love the word yes. I know that yes sounds much more polite than no, but sometimes we need to say no and it's OK. This is a really good topic to discuss with your parents and together decide the different reasons you might want to say no. Let me tell you why I say no, and then you and your parents or class can discuss other reasons we might want to use the no word. I say no, when someone asks me to do something I am not comfortable with. Sometimes other people have different standards from mine and ask me to participate in an activity that I do not feel good about. In this case, I say no. Of course, I usually try to use my manners when saying no, so that I don't make others feel like I'm judging them. I may say something like, "No thank you. I'm not comfortable with that." I also say no when someone asks to borrow something that is extremely special to me. For instance, if someone were to ask to borrow my book on famous ghost stories that my grandpa gave to me (he also wrote me a special note and signed it inside the front cover), I would say, "No, I'm sorry, but I don't lend that book out because it means too much to me." It's OK to say no; just try to be polite and compassionate when you use this word. And remember, respect others when they tell you no and hopefully our no's will be respected too. See you next time.

Activity
Discuss with the class some possible reasons we might use the word no. No is a powerful word that many children are uncomfortable saying. It's important that all children gain confidence in using the word no. The best way to encourage this is to practice. Set up many situations and allow the children to practice saying no. This can be very empowering.

Day 17
1st Request

What does "1st Request" mean?

It means that we obey and respond on someone's first request, mainly those of our parents and our teachers. Why is first request so important and why is it considered proper etiquette? Well remember, if etiquette means helping others feel valued, then honoring our parents' request the first time they ask, shows that we value their authority and them. If someone just ignores us when we ask them something, we can feel hurt, anger, mistrust and we wonder whether we are valued by this individual. Has your mom ever said, "Honey, will you please come and take out the trash?" You respond, "OK Mom." However, twenty minutes go by and you have still not taken out the trash. In fact, you've forgotten about it. Then your mom more angrily says, "I thought I asked you to take out the trash. Why do I always have to ask more than once to get you to do anything?" Does this exchange sound kind of familiar? You may be thinking that really, this isn't that big a deal. So what if my mom has to ask me more than once to do something? Eventually, I get it done. Well, actually, it is a big deal. The reason it's a big deal is because when we don't respond immediately to our parent's or teacher's request, we are sending them a message that we really don't value their word, their time, or them. We're actually behaving rudely and being disobedient to those who love and care about us the most. Our leaders, teachers and parents, hopefully have our best interest at heart. They want what is best for us. They want us to succeed, be happy and be productive. This is the basis for why they lead, guide and direct you in the way they do. Show your respect, your love, and your appreciation for them by obeying their first request. It's a great way to exhibit polite manners.

Activity

Make a real effort to obey your parents' first request this week. After the week is over, sit down with parents and children and discuss this experience. Was it a good experience? Did feelings of love and peace increase in the home? Commit to continue to strive to obey first request. A reward system is always a fun way to reward obedience and effort.

Day 18
Empathy

Empathy is a great gift to have, one in which would benefit all mankind if we all tried to have more of it. So what is it? Empathy is the ability to feel what someone else is feeling or to understand why someone is feeling a certain way. Have you ever wondered what it might feel like to be homeless? I've seen individual make fun of homeless people, because their clothes were dirty and dingy and they looked quite unkempt. When I see this kind of behavior, it makes me very sad. I wonder if those who make fun of the homeless have ever stopped and wondered what it must feel like to not have a home. What does it feel like to only own one or two outfits? What does it feel like to not have a place to feel safe from the world? I would imagine that none of us can understand what it does feel like, unless we have experienced it ourselves. Even though we might not ever be homeless, we can try to imagine what it might feel like. When we do this simple exercise in our minds, it encourages us to have more compassion for those in that situation. This is what empathy is. It's trying to imagine yourself in "someone else's shoes". It helps us to have more understanding and compassion for others. It helps to prevent us from judging others. The next time you see someone sad or even mad, try to imagine what this person is feeling and why. Doing this, will help you make better decisions when dealing with others. I hope we can all become more empathetic with one another, I know I will try harder. See you next time.

Activity
Today, I want your mom and your dad to write down their normal daily schedule. These schedules should include everything they are responsible for in a normal day. It would be most effective if they were recorded in 30 minute or 1 hour increments. Next, allow the family to review both schedules. As the children consider what it's like to "walk in their parents' shoes", hopefully there will be more feelings of appreciation and understanding by the children, especially when help is requested. Discuss the benefits of trying to put ourselves in "others' shoes".

Day 19
Sharing

I know, I know. You're thinking, "Shouldn't this subject be discussed with toddlers, who have trouble sharing their toys?" Well yes, that's where it begins, but actually we continue to have opportunities to share well beyond the toddler years. The trouble with getting older and sharing is that as we age, our toys usually become more expensive, and it's not as easy to share them. Instead of toy trucks and dolls, we've got I-pods and cell phones. None of us want to be considered selfish or stingy; we would rather be thought of as giving and generous. My advice is to share as often as you can, but discuss with your parents those items that are not appropriate to share. One thing I know we can all share is our time. Our time is very valuable, so as we take the time to help someone else with a problem, or go and visit someone who is sick or afflicted, we are sharing ourselves, which is a great thing to share. We can be generous with our time, with our talents, with our attention and with our things as a way of showing others we care. It's really fun to share. I'm sure you have felt both the satisfaction and happiness when someone shares something with you, but I'm also sure you have felt the disappointment when someone has refused to share with you. Try to keep those feelings in mind, the next time you have the opportunity to share. See you next time.

Activity
This week, take the opportunity to go and visit someone who is sick, or can't get out much or who is in need of a visit for any reason. Discuss with your family someone who would benefit from such a visit. Taking a treat such as cookies or a flower is always great fun. Enjoy sharing your time!

Day 20
Borrowing

Have you ever borrowed something from someone, say a book, video game or clothes? Well, I'm sure you have. I know I have borrowed many things in my life. I must admit I haven't always been as responsible as I should have when it came to borrowing, but now I try really hard. Let me help you become a "responsible borrower". You might think it's not that important, but trust me when I say that I have seen friendships ruined over borrowing. Here are the borrowing rules:

1. Politely ask before you take.
2. Receive permission before you take.
3. Inform the lender when you plan on returning the item.
4. Treat the item with extreme care, so you can return it in the same condition that you borrowed it.
5. Never lend to others anything that is not yours.
6. Return items on time, and in good condition, and in person (don't ask another friend to return the item).
7. Thank the lender for their generosity and remind them that you look forward to returning the favor sometime.

It's really important that you remember these borrowing rules. This allows people to trust you and know that you keep your word. Be careful what you borrow and try not to abuse someone's generosity by asking to borrow too often. Good luck. See you next time.

Activity
Grab a Jump rope and try to jump as you say this rhyme:

I Like to Borrow, because it's fun;
If no permission, I better run.
I treat the item with great care
And always return it, unless I dare
I thank the lender because it's nice
I like to share, sometimes even twice

Day 21
Eating—A Time to be with Friends and Family

I love eating! I hope you enjoy it too. Did you know that there are really two reasons we eat? Sure, one is to actually put food into our mouths so we will have the energy to continue our day, but there is another important reason we sit down to eat: to socialize. What does that mean? Well, socializing is when we communicate with others. I love sitting down with my family or friends and catching up on the day's events or what's going on in everyone's lives. Sitting around a table while we're eating is the perfect place to reconnect with those we care about and love. Why? Well for one thing, everyone has to eat. So you know that everyone has to stop what they're doing at least three times a day and put some food in their mouths. Why not take advantage of this small time

each day when our day sort of "freezes", and reconnect with one another? Because this is a great time to socialize, we, of course, have to consider some rules about the whole process. If sitting down and eating is the perfect time to talk to others, how are we supposed to do that with proper etiquette, when we're not supposed to eat and talk at the same time? Sounds difficult, but in fact it's really not. With a few simple rules and just some basic knowledge of proper dining etiquette, we're going to be able to really enjoy these special opportunities and help make sure that everyone with us enjoys this time together also. Are you ready? Here we go! See you next time.

Activity
This week, schedule at least one dinner that your whole family can enjoy together. Dinner time is not the time to worry about correcting everyone's manners, but a time to reconnect with one another. Everyone at the dinner table has to answer two questions:

#1 When I daydream, I like to think about………..

#2 If I could snap my finger and be anyone in the world for just one day, I would be…. Have fun sharing your thoughts with your family.

Day 22
Never Allow Others to Sit Alone

The first etiquette rule on dining is this: Never allow others to sit alone. Let's remember when we discussed empathy and use that skill to imagine what it would feel like if you were sitting alone, eating your lunch, while beside you was a table full of kids who were laughing and talking and having a wonderful time. You would feel pretty lonely and maybe even embarrassed that you were alone. Well I know that we're starting to get the "hang of it" with regards to what etiquette means, so I also realize you're already ahead of me and know just what to do in this particular situation. Yes, invite the person to join you. "Hey, John, would you like to come sit with us?" What if, however, there are only 8 chairs at your table, and there are already 8 of you at the table? Well, hopefully, everyone can scoot over a little and make room for one more. If not, I hope you have the courage to say to your friends, "Hey, guys, you know I love eating with you, but today I'm going to eat with John so he doesn't have to eat alone."   Can you imagine how that would make John feel? And not only would you please John, but what an example you would be to your friends. I know that every act of kindness that is witnessed by others produces more acts of kindness. It's a universal law, I'm sure of it. Try it and feel good. See you next time.

Activity
Play the "Friend, Do You Want to Join Us?" Game. How do you play? The group forms a circle, placing one person inside the circle. The person inside circle picks a person from the circle who approaches the person inside the circle and says, "Friend, would you like to join us in the circle?" Other person responds by saying, "Friend, I would love to join you in the circle, but I just can't smile." While this person is responding, the person from the circle is making funny faces, funny noises, trying to get the person inside the circle to laugh. If they laugh, they can't join the circle. If they don't laugh, then the person trying to make them laugh takes their place inside the circle. Continue play.

Day 23
Eating at School (or with other children)

Whether you go to school or are home schooled, I'm sure sometimes you find yourselves in groups of children eating lunch together. I know, it's really fun. It sometimes can get kind of "crazy" when a bunch of children get together and try to have a meal. I guess that's one reason it is fun. Regardless, please allow me to make a few suggestions since we're discussing proper etiquette. The same basic rules still apply such as; chew with mouth closed, don't talk with food in mouth, no loud noises, and keep hands to yourselves. A few other things to think about are: make sure you wash your hands before you eat. Our hands usually are the dirtiest part of our body, so it is always smart to wash your hands or use a sanitizer before you eat. Also, I know kids like to share things. I remember we talked about being generous and giving. Sharing food is a little different, however. When we touch food with our hands or even our mouths (like sipping on a straw), our germs, whether they be good germs or unhealthy germs, are passed to whatever we touch. That's why it's not always a good idea to share food and drinks. If you do share, be careful with your handling of the food or drink. Try not to make a habit of sharing food or asking others to share their food.

Some people are really uncomfortable sharing food, but they don't want others to think they are selfish. The best rule is simply not to ask. Remember to clean up your area and place trash in the proper places. Enjoy your friends and practice polite manners so that all who are present will enjoy their meal, too.

Activity
Now is a great time to review how germs are transferred from one person to another. Emphasize the importance of washing hands thoroughly before eating and after visiting the restroom. Discuss places of concern where we need to be especially careful and diligent when trying to stay germ free (like public restrooms, doctors' waiting rooms, etc.).

Day 24
Setting the Table

Ah, the setting of the table. This sounds overwhelming but, hopefully, this lesson will help you remember a few "setting" rules that work for most everyone. First of all, we like to set the plates at a reasonable distance apart. This means not too far and not too close. If they're too far apart, it will make it hard to have conversation and make it difficult to pass things to one another. If they're too close, people's arms, legs and elbows get in the way with each other. So keep this in mind. Now, I'm not going to teach you how to set the table for a fourteen course meal. How often does that happen in our lives? These are instructions for a typical table setting that would be

appropriate in most any home, whether for two people or for a dinner party for ten. If you need more formal instruction, there are lots and lots of books on formal table settings that would be fitting to serve the Queen. For the rest of us, here it goes: The dinner plate is on the table, centered to the chair. A salad plate is set on top of the dinner plate. The napkin is simply folded and placed on top of the salad plate. The knives are set to the right of the plate with the cutting edge facing towards the plate. You may set one or two knives, depending on whether you have more than one course that requires a knife. If soup is being served, then a soup spoon is placed on the outside of the knives. The forks are placed on the left side of the plate, with the salad fork being on the outside and main entrée fork being closest to the plate. The way you distinguish between a salad fork and an entrée fork is the number and size of tines ("pointy things on the fork"). The one with shorter or fewer tines, is the salad fork. A water goblet (glass) is placed above the top right of the plate (at 1:00 if your plate were a clock). That's it. Not so hard, is it? Look at the picture on this page and hopefully it will be clearer. Sometimes more than one beverage is served, which requires more glasses. Unique courses, such as appetizers, sometimes require different plates and utensils. However, this is a basic place setting and if you get this much right when you set the table for your family, I'm sure they will be very impressed. Now go home and impress your mom when you volunteer to set the table tonight, and she sees the beautiful result. See you next time.

Activity
Awesome Game to Play: This game is really fun when you have at least 6 to play, so get the whole family involved. Get two bags. In each bag place a complete table setting including napkins, plates, utensils and cups. Divide into two teams. Each team will line up behind their leader. The first person from each team will race to a table when the "whistle" blows and set their place setting appropriately. When their setting is "OK'd" by the referee, then they bag everything up again and race back to the next person on their team and then the race continues. The first team to finish is the winning team. Good Luck!

Day 25
More Polite Table Setting Suggestions

1. Use small glass bowls instead of plastic bottles for condiments (ketchup, mustard, relish, etc.) Instead of putting the bottle of ketchup on the table, place the ketchup in a small bowl with a small serving spoon. You may do the same with any condiment, including pickles, beets, olives, etc.

2. Make sure your silverware is clean and free from spots. All it takes to shine silverware is a piece of clean cloth. You can wipe away soap spots or smudges and have beautiful silverware that your guests aren't afraid to use.

3. Provide one salt-and-pepper shaker for every four people at the table. For instance, if there are six people at the table, there should be two sets of salt-and-pepper shakers, etc. This simply prevents anyone from having to wait too long to use the salt-and-pepper. Remember, etiquette is always trying to help people feel more comfortable.

4. Centerpieces are always a fun way to help create a more attractive table. Just remember that your centerpiece should not be so high that it would hinder two people sitting across the table from one another from being able to see each other easily. Also, make sure the centerpiece is clean and free from dust. Candles are also pretty, but sometimes lit candles put off an odor that a guest may not enjoy. Try to use unscented candles.

These suggestions may seem too fancy to do if it's just you and your family having dinner. I believe nothing is too fancy for our family and sometimes going to a little extra trouble for our immediate family helps remind us all that every time we're with our family is a special time. See you next time.

Activity
Create a table centerpiece. If a special holiday is near, create a holiday centerpiece. Get creative and search for household items that you can put together to form something really unique. Have fun and let everyone use their creativity.

Day 26
Table Linens

Table linens include placemats and table cloths that are used to decorate and protect the table. It is our job to be careful when handling table linens and to be extra careful when eating on table linens. Basically, we just need to do our best to keep the linens clean and free from careless spills. You're probably thinking like I am and wondering, "So why do we use table linens when we're eating if we're not supposed to get them dirty?" Doesn't make real good sense, does it? Well, guess what? I don't have all the answers. I just know that someone long ago decided table linens made tables more attractive, so that's what we do. They also can protect some tables, especially those made of wood, from water stains or burn spots from hot plates. Regardless, they are used and we need to be respectful of them. I know I have some tablecloths that were my great grandmother's and I like to use them when my family comes to dinner, just so we can have a memory of my great grandma while we are all together. They are very special to me. A good rule to help keep these table linens clean and in good condition is to not place dirty utensils directly on the linens. Do not use a table linen to wipe up anything. When serving yourself and others from the serving bowls, be careful to not make spills. If ever you do have an accident with regard to a table linen, quickly ask the host there is a special way they would like you to clean up the accident. Accidents do happen. It's not the end of the world, but do be considerate of the linens and all will be fine. See you next time.

Activity
Find something in your house that used to belong to one of your ancestors or ask your parents what your family has that used to belong to one of your ancestors. Look at the item and have your mom or dad tell you what they know about the item and a little about the ancestor who once owned it. As we learn the history of special heirlooms, we come to appreciate them and we want to honor them by tenderly caring for them.

Day 27
Using Your Napkin

Napkins are a part of table linens, but these linens are allowed to be personally used. Napkins are not for taking a bath or washing all the baseball dirt off your face before you start to eat. They are used for "dabbing". Dabbing is using the napkin to gently touch your mouth where there might be food or the remains of a beverage. NO SCRUBBING WITH THE NAPKIN! Upon sitting down to dine, you take your napkin, fold it in half and place it on your lap. This is where your napkin remains until it is time to leave the table. If you have to be excused from the table for a short length of time, fold the napkin in half and place it on your seat. Your dining napkin is never used to blow your nose or to hold unwanted food items. Remember, etiquette is always thinking of others. Can you imagine the waitress or your host coming to clear the table and, upon picking up your napkin, seeing some unpleasant item fall out of it?....Yuck! This would not be very gracious to your waiter or your host. It's also not very polite to tuck your napkin into your shirt, regardless of what you may have seen your uncle do. And remember; never use the tablecloth as a napkin. This is a big "no, no"! See you next time.

Activity
It's time to play "Musical Chairs". This time however, we're going to use our napkins. Line the chairs up and place a folded napkin in each chair. When the music stops, the child has to sit down, placing the napkin properly in his/her lap. When the music starts again, the child stands, folds the napkin in half and place back on the seat. Have fun!

Day 28
Sitting Politely at Table

I remember when I was around ten years old and I was a flower girl in a wedding. My cousin was the ring bearer. We had to attend the rehearsal dinner which was at a very nice restaurant, and both my mom and my cousin's mom were so worried that my cousin and I would embarrass them. Can you believe that? Well, all I remember is that my cousin decided to be a little stinker, just to get our moms in a tizzy, so he started eating his salad with his fingers. I started laughing so loud that I couldn't sit still in my chair. I'll never forget the looks on my mom's and my aunt's faces: priceless. I wouldn't recommend that behavior in the future.

You know, it's hard to sit still and sit quietly at a table. Kids tend to be little "wiggle worms"; even when they get to middle school, they have a hard time being still. All that energy is a good thing. You'll use it for lots of great reasons, but part of growing up or maturing is learning how to control all of our energy and use it at the right times. I have found that when children are really involved in the dinner conversation, they have a much easier time sitting still, and they enjoy the meal time much more. Have you ever asked your parents how their day was? A great question to ask your parent is, "Who was your favorite teacher when you were a kid and why?", or, "Did you and your friends have a special place you went to play? What was it like and where was it?" Listening to stories about your parents' childhood is a great way to get to know your parents better. I would encourage you to think of ways to have better conversation at your dinner table that you and the whole family will enjoy. Try it…it's fun. See you next time.

Activity
Make a list of ten questions you can ask your other family members to get to know them better. Keep this list handy while you eat dinner this week. Once you have learned all the answers, make a new list of questions. Sometimes we need "conversation starters" to help us have ideas about what to talk about. This is perfectly OK. As we get to know our family better, we will enjoy dinner time much more. Enjoy!

Day 29
Thanking and Complimenting the Cook

Thanking and complimenting the cook is an essential part of proper etiquette. Before we ever take our first bite, it is polite to find a compliment to say that expresses our gratitude to the cook for the time and energy it took to prepare and serve our meal. Something like, "Wow Grandma, the table and food look absolutely beautiful. I can't wait to dig-in. It doesn't matter how old someone is, or how often they complete a certain task; everyone likes their efforts to be recognized, even your mom. Have you ever worked really hard on something like cleaning your room, writing a paper, or completing a piece of artwork, but no one seems to recognize or appreciate the effort you put in? It doesn't feel that good, does it? Well, believe it or not, your parents and even all adults are no different from you. We all like sincere compliments. It's also important to remember that proper etiquette means you NEVER, NEVER, NEVER complain about what is being served at the table. It might not be your favorite meal; in fact it might be that you would rather sleep with snakes than eat that meal; however, we do not make those thoughts known, especially to the cook. We use

tact. We look for positive things we can comment on. We enjoy the foods we like, we try everything, and we find ways to show appreciation for the cook, always being sensitive to the feelings of those who serve us. See you next time.

Activity
One of the best ways to say "thank you" to the one who normally prepares the meals in your home, is to give them a day off. Talk to your siblings, father or other members of the family and plan a meal that the rest of you can prepare completely, without the help of the one who normally prepares the meals. The one, who normally prepares the meals, gets to be the queen or king of the table and everyone else cooks and serves them. Have fun with this and make sure the king or queen knows that this is your thank you to them for always making great meals.

Day 30
Wait.........

OK, I'll admit it. This is sometimes hard to do. However, this is very important. When eating with others, we don't begin to eat until everyone is seated and has been served. It is rude to begin enjoying all the wonderful food while others, who are just as hungry as you, are still waiting for their food to be served. I realize there is a chance your food might not remain as hot as you would like, but putting other's feelings above our own is the ultimate act of good manners. Sometimes on occasion, someone still waiting for their meal will tell everyone to please go ahead and eat. In this instance, you may use your best judgment. If you are at a large gathering, where there may be many tables set up for people, you only need to wait until everyone at your immediate table is seated and served. I know your thoughtfulness and consideration will be much appreciated. Your character (personal traits) is continuing to grow and improve as you attempt to apply these etiquette considerations to your life. It takes time. Don't be discouraged but enjoy learning, growing and maturing as you add more "tools" into your "building arsenal". See you next time.

Activity
This is called the "Waiting Game". Someone starts out by describing what he/she is, and the other people try to guess what they're describing. For example, someone could say, "I am big; I love to give myself a shower with my special shower dispenser. Watch out, because if I step on you, you won't like it. Gray is my favorite color. What am I?" Four clues should be given. The other people guess and whoever guesses right, gets to be the next one to describe their imaginative self, (an elephant of course was the answer). You can be an animal or an object, just not other people. We don't want to hurt anyone's feelings.

Day 31
Dining Considerations

There are a few dining considerations that I wanted to mention. I'm sure you are aware that many of us share different beliefs, customs and traditions. As we visit our friends' homes, we see that not everyone does things the way our family does. This is what makes our world so charming. It is polite to always honor the traditions and customs of the family you are visiting. If you're at your friend's house and they say a blessing before they dine, but you usually do not say a blessing, you would simply participate as a show of respect for that family. The opposite could happen as well. You may be at a friend's house who's family does not pray at meal time; once again, honoring their family is always the polite thing to do. This does not mean you cannot participate in your own customs; however, be careful that as a guest, you are not imposing your beliefs on those you visit.

Second, remember when we sit at a table, our feet are supposed to be on the ground (if they do not reach the ground, they should still face forward) and our chair should remain still throughout the meal. This means no rocking, leaning back or any type of noise or disruption should take place. We are always trying to be respectful, not only to the people around us, but also to the furniture we are using.

When you are finished eating, always push your chair in and offer to help with the clean-up. Even if you're sure the host will not allow you to help, always, always offer. Make sure you are familiar with the clean-up process, in case someone ever "takes you up" on your offer.

See you next time.

Activity
If your children haven't practiced this yet, now is a great time to go over the steps in cleaning up dishes and the kitchen. Review the proper way to discard uneaten food, wipe down condiments that must be returned to the refrigerator, stack a dishwasher and wipe down tables and countertops. These are lifetime skills that require practice. Maybe it's not a favorite activity, but it's absolutely necessary.

Day 32
Buffet Lines

After I tell you this next etiquette rule, you students are going to start wondering if I'm ever going to give you some good news. You're going to have to trust me when I say that there is a HUGE payoff for adding these etiquette skills to your life. You'll probably never realize how much good will come into your life as a direct result of acquiring these tools, but they will come. They will. Buffets are a fun way to eat. Most people like going to buffets because of the variety and amount of food you may eat. Here are some considerations for buffet lines:

1. Whenever you are attending a party, reunion or social get-together that includes a buffet line, remember the line should form from oldest to youngest. Any time we can pay respect and show consideration for older persons we should do so. Insist that those older than you go first.

2. Take moderate size portions. We always want to make sure that the food doesn't run out before the last guest is served. Be considerate of those behind you and only take moderate portions. You can always go back for seconds once everyone has been served.

3. Use only serving utensils when getting food, not your personal silverware.

4. Do not take a dirty plate back to the buffet for seconds. Always get a clean plate.

5. Do not eat while standing at the buffet line (food could fall from your mouth into serving dishes). Enjoy a buffet line, but remember these considerations so everyone can enjoy the experience. See you next time.

Activity
In a conversation, discuss the buffet line rules. Name the rules and tell why they are important.

Day 33
Passing the Food

When everyone is seated at the table and it is time to start passing the food, a few considerations can help make this a smooth process. Sometimes families like to just send everything around in one big circle. Usually the passing should start with the meat and then proceed to the left. Since more people are right handed than left handed, most people will hold a serving dish in their left hand and use their right hand for serving. Before you pass the serving plate, make sure it is not too hot; be sure to warn the next guest if it is warm. Once again, moderate portions are polite. Even though the only thing on the table that you think you like is the mac-n-cheese, this does not mean that you help yourself to 6 portion sizes of mac-n-cheese and nothing else. This would not be considerate of the other guests who wanted the mac-n-cheese before it all ended up on your plate. If things are being passed on an as needed basis, simply ask, "May I please have some potatoes?" or "Will you please pass the gravy?" If a plate is too heavy, ask an adult to help you. It is not worth the risk of spilling the contents of a serving dish all over the table. If someone asks for the salt, make sure you pass the salt and the pepper. If you are the host, it's always polite to ask if everyone has everything they need. You may make some suggestions of things guest might want, such as butter, relish, ketchup or salsa. Good Luck! See you next time.

Activity
As with all these etiquette considerations, the best way to learn them is to practice. Sit around the table with several empty bowls and platters and simply practice passing and serving food. When you're passing a basket of bread for instance, it's polite to hold the basket while your neighbor takes a piece. Then hand your neighbor the basket so they may pass it. If it's a heavy or hot dish, simply place it beside your neighbor and allow them to serve themselves. Sometimes it's easiest for the host to serve a certain dish if it's simply to messy or heavy to pass around the dinner table. Have fun passing.

Day 34
Correct Use of Utensils

Holding our utensils correctly is an important part of using proper manners at the dinner table. When holding our utensils, we never want to hold them in a way that appears we are in fear of someone taking them away from us. This might send a message to others that we don't trust them around our precious utensils. So, remember to hold them firmly, yet with some gentleness. I'll explain. But first, let me give you some utensil definitions. The blade of a knife is considered to be the sharp side of a knife. The tines of a fork are the points that we stick into things. So with that said, once we have used a utensil, never place it back on the table; remember, we want to keep the table linens clean. You should place used utensils only on your plate. When you simply want to lay your utensils down for a moment, while you chat or to take a sip of water, it is best to lay the knife and fork flat on the plate with tips pointing towards each other (at 5:00 and 7:00) and tines facing up. This signifies that you are taking a rest but you are still eating. When you are finished with your meal and are ready for your plate to be removed, lay your fork and knife side by side at the bottom of your plate with the handles hanging slightly over at 4:00 and tips pointing towards 11:00 and tines facing up. This signifies that you are ready for your plate to be cleared or that you are simply finished. Please try not to clang your utensils, using them as drums or swords or in any other distracting manner. You're learning a lot. Great job! See you next time.

Activity
Practice makes perfect here. With plastic utensils and plastic plates, let the children practice properly holding utensils and setting them down to signal they are taking a break or are finished with their meal.

Day 35
The American Style of Dining

Yes, believe it or not, we Americans do have our own style of eating. Of course, it's very polite to learn about the dining customs of other countries before you visit them, so as not to violate their traditions. Investigating other countries' dining customs would be a great homework assignment for you and your family. For now, we're going to concentrate on the American Style of Dining. We begin by cutting bite size portions of food. This means the food must fit into your mouth without its looking like you have a "jaw breaker" in your cheek. We cut one bite at a time by piercing the food with our fork, tines facing down and pointer finger on the back of the fork. We place the knife in our dominant hand with pointer finger pressing down on the knife. When we're cutting, we should not be able to see the ends of our utensils because they should be covered by our hands. We then gently "saw" our food with our elbows in by our bodies. We then lay our knife on the side of our plate and switch the fork to our dominant hand with tines facing up, and remove the food with our lips (never our teeth). We go through this process each time we need to cut a bite. It's not polite to eat all of one food item on your plate before eating the rest of the items. The proper way is to rotate between the food items. It's OK if while we're young, our parents cut up all our food for us, but as we age, we will practice the proper way. When not cutting, place the knife on the side of your plate with the blade facing in. This style of eating is once again called the American Style of Dining. Most of you probably already eat like this without ever being told that this is actually a style. If it sounds a little complicated or different from what you're used to, just practice when it doesn't count. Get a piece of bread and pretend that it's a steak, and, with a few other food items, simply practice with others. It can be quite fun.

See you next time.

Activity
Now is definitely the time to sit at the table with your children and practice cutting food. Get a piece of sandwich bread and let your children practice cutting and eating. This takes time and practice.

Day 36
Serving and Buttering Bread

Yes, we have etiquette rules regarding buttering bread. Listen, I know you're not going to be perfect at all these dining rules instantly. They take practice. In reality, grown-ups don't expect children to be perfect at dining etiquette. But as long as we're making progress and slowly trying to incorporate these etiquette skills into our lives, then we are doing great. You don't just become an adult, and suddenly you're perfect at everything. Good habits take time to form, and, by starting when you're young, it will be so much easier than trying to correct bad habits when you're older. Believe me when I say that adults don't always take to change very well. Learn while you're young. Now as for bread etiquette, just a few considerations: first, we usually wait to place bread plates on the table once the hot bread has arrived. However, sometimes it's simply easier to go ahead and set the bread plates. Bread plates are brought in at the same time the bread is brought in, and then, the bread plate is placed to the top left of the dinner plate. Second, usually a basket or plate of bread is passed around.   Hold the bread basket for your neighbor and ask, "Would you care for any bread?" After they take the bread from the basket and place it on their bread plate, then you may pass the basket to them for them to then pass. It's proper to "break bread" instead of cutting bread. Thirdly, once you have your bread, use the butter knife to cut a small piece of butter from the butter bowl and place it on the side of your bread plate. Return the butter knife. You will then use your own knife to butter your bread from the butter on your plate. That's all. Easy, right? See you next time.

Activity
Once again, the best activity for the etiquette skill is to practice. Get a basket of bread and practice breaking bread, passing bread, placing butter on the bread plate and buttering bread. As you practice these skills, your children will gain confidence and be more at ease when dining in front of others. It also helps us parents to not be so nervous when taking our children in public to dine. Enjoy!

Day 37
Removing "Unwanted Items"

This isn't the easiest subject to talk about but it must be addressed. What do you do when you realize there is something in your mouth when you are eating that should not be there (hair, rock, bone, foreign object)? The most polite way to handle this is to remove the item using your first finger (pointer finger) and your thumb as discreetly as possible and then place it on the side of your plate. If you do not wish to look at the object or do not wish others to see the object, you may lay a paper napkin over the top of it. This type of behavior should only be exercised in extreme situations in which you are simply not capable of swallowing the object that is in your mouth. However, if you simply do not like the taste of something, you still must swallow it. It is extremely rude to spit out the contents of your mouth, regardless of what it tastes like. And absolutely without exception, NEVER, NEVER, NEVER spit food into your dinner napkin. Remember, we don't like to leave unexpected gifts for our host. OK. That's all I'll say about that. I think you understand. Best of luck with these situations. You're going to need it. See you next time.

Activity
Get some small candy like jelly beans, some hot tamales or some M&Ms. Have the children practice removing these items discreetly from their mouth. The trick here is to do this without laughing. This is a fun activity. After a few tries, have fun eating your candy.

Day 38
Forks or Fingers?

Yes, there are many foods we love to eat with our fingers (corn on the cob, french fries, burgers, pork ribs, fried chicken legs, etc.). The rule here is this: If you can't eat it without smearing food all over you, your hands or your face then you must eat it with a fork. It's that simple. There cannot be food dripping down your arms or any other area. This would be a clear sign that you should be using a fork. I realize that eatin some of these items is more "an experience" than just a meal, but please realize that others usually do not find it very appealing to watch someone eating while juices are smeared on their face and running down their arms. Remembering our definition of etiquette (making others feel comfortable), we have to consider the dining experience of those around us. If you simply must eat with your hands, make sure you have plenty of napkins to keep yourself clean and tidy. Have fun eating those ribs. See you next time.

Day 39
Accidents at the Table

It happens to everyone. We've all done it and I'm sure we're going to do it again before too long. The best way to prevent accidents from happening at the table is to be cautious when moving items and to sit relatively still while at the table. Never be in too big a hurry. This is when spills most often occur. Take your time when pouring your drink or passing food, and never reach across others or across the table to retrieve something, instead, always ask for items to be passed to you. If an accident does occur, move quickly to clean it up. Never just look up at the host or even your mom and say, "Mom, I spilled my milk." Instead, quickly get something to wipe up the milk and continue to clean it up until the mess is COMPLETELY cleaned up. We are all very capable of cleaning up our own messes. Never expect others to clean up our messes. Apologize to the other guests at the table, and then forget about it. It was just an accident and there's no sense in spending any further time discussing the why's, how's and what-if's of it. If your accident was such that it might have ruined or stained a table linen, you may want to offer to have it professionally cleaned or even pay for a replacement. Use your best judgment. See you next time.

Activity
Have a discussion about the difference in careless behavior at the table and a true accident. Accidents happen to everyone. Sometimes it's important for all of us to have things put into prospectus. It's not necessary that any of us dwell on or spend unnecessary time, discussing why or how an accident occurred. Remind your children that there are big accidents and small accidents and an accident at the table is definitely a small accident. We apologize, we clean it up and then we forget about it.

Day 40
Taking the Last Bite

Have you ever been "eyeing" the last piece of chocolate pie and wondering whether you should go for it or not. Well, it's OK if you do, but the polite thing is to ask if anyone else would like it, before you take it. For instance, "If no one is going to eat this last piece of pie, I would love to have it," or, "I would be willing to share." Most people, unless it's your brother, are going to say, "No, you go ahead and enjoy it." People appreciate so much your willingness to ask before you take, that they usually allow you to have it, even though they might love it themselves. This rule applies to everything, whether it's the last piece of cake, the last piece of pizza, or the last piece of gum. It's amazing the payoffs that happen when we use proper etiquette. Another consideration is asking for seconds. Remember, that when you're in your own home, it is perfectly polite to ask if you may have seconds. However, when you are a guest in someone's home, it is impolite to ask for seconds; wait until you're offered seconds and then it's perfectly OK. See you next time.

Day 41
Don't Forget....

Yes, you're almost finished with dining etiquette. You've done great! It's been a lot of information, but I know that you are going to be successful using your new etiquette skills at the table, and others are going to notice and appreciate your polite dining manners. Here are a few final considerations I want to mention before we move on:

Remember, we try not to make any unattractive noises while eating, such as slurping, sipping, sucking, chomping, smacking, tapping, etc. Basically, any noise that would distract others while they are eating or trying to have conversation would not be polite.

We also do our best to be on our best behavior while at the dinner table, which includes avoiding such things as whining, interrupting, fussing, fidgeting, eating with our mouths open, talking with food in our mouths and disobedience. These types of behaviors would not be considered polite.

Lastly, we always want to ask to be excused when we are finished with our meal. An example of this might be, "Dad, Mom, I really enjoyed this dinner. May I please be excused?" After you are excused and have cleared your own dishes, always ask the host, "May I help you clean up the dishes?"

Wow, we're done. I hope you have learned a lot about dining etiquette. Mostly however, I hope you have learned skills that are going to make your dining experience more enjoyable for you, as well as for those you are with. Remember to enjoy meal time. It is a special time to be with family and friends. Good job! See you next time.

Activity

Now it's time to practice everything. Let the whole family plan and prepare a special meal with all the "fixins". Allow the children to set a beautiful table with linens and a centerpiece. Practice all your new skills. Be sure to be positive and give encouragement. Dinner time is a time to enjoy but this particular time is considered "practice". This is the time to be able to make mistakes and be gently corrected without feeling embarrassed. Enjoy the family!

Day 42
Relax at Dinner Time

Although many of our etiquette skills revolve around the dinner table, a word of caution to the whole family: we don't want dinner time to become a time of lecture and discipline. Dinner time should be something the whole family looks forward to. It's a time to catch up on everyone's day: a time to tell funny stories and talk about history, the day's news or concerns of any family members. It's a time to bond with one another. So while we're actually dining, it's OK to bring up one etiquette skill to remember, but only one. Children should not be "riding" each other on all the mistakes they're making, and parents should not be critiquing every move a child makes. The more we demonstrate to our children these etiquette skills, the more they will watch, learn, and act appropriately. If a parent notices an extremely rude behavior at the dinner table and wishes to correct it immediately, the polite way to handle this is to ask for you and your child to be excused for a moment, so as not to embarrass the child. As we look for ways to show respect to our children, our children's desire to please us will increase and the result will be more obedience and more love shared between us and our children. See you next time.

Activity
It's time for your family or your class to start collecting "warm fuzzies". Allow me to tell you how. Get a really large jar. Buy a bag of multi colored "pom-poms" from the craft store. The rule is that anyone in the family or the class can give a "warm fuzzy" to anyone else. "Warm fuzzies" are placed in the jar when someone in the family or the class witnesses someone else in the family or the class practicing an etiquette skill. The goal is to fill up the jar with "warm fuzzies". When the jar is completely full, have a party. A "Warm Fuzzy" party. Be creative and just have fun!

Day 43
Attending Parties

I love parties! Who doesn't? Going to a party is always fun and exciting. Whether it's a birthday party, a special holiday or just a family get-together, it's fun to be with our friends and family and just have fun. My favorite kind of party is a birthday party, because I love birthday cake, birthday presents, and I love taking pictures with my camera. What's your favorite kind of party? Yes, your own birthday party counts. Has your mom ever told you right before you get out of the car as you're being delivered to a party, "Make sure you're on your best behavior."? I bet she has. So what is our best behavior? I know of people whose best behavior is probably the same as another's worst behavior. In general however, when we consider the best way to behave, we would probably all agree on a few things such as these:

- No rough play or running in someone's house
- Keep our feet off the furniture
- Eat and drink only in designated rooms
- Stay out of rooms which have closed doors
- No opening people's refrigerators or cabinets and drawers without permission
- If we make a spill, tell an adult quickly and help clean up
- Participate in all activities
- No complaining
- Enjoy everyone's company

These are a few ways to ensure that our behavior will be acceptable to the host and that we are respecting the home of those we are visiting.

Activity
Discuss these ideas with your family or class and think of other ways to exemplify best behavior. Good Luck. See you next time.

Day 44
Party Invitations

Isn't it exciting when you get a letter in the mail? You'd better enjoy it while you're young. Young people seem to get party invitations and birthday cards in the mail which is always so much fun, but we adults usually get a lot of bills and junk in the mail. Oh well, I still love getting party invitations and from the minute I receive the invitation, I start getting excited about attending the party. It's more polite to mail your invitations rather than handing them out in person. This way, we don't cause those who don't get an invitation to feel uncomfortable. We never want to hurt others' feelings, especially when it can be avoided by being more discreet. Invitations usually have information on them that tells us important details regarding the party, such as this:

- Who it's for
- The date and time it begins
- Where it's going to be
- Sometimes it will tell us how to dress
- Finally, it will say RSVP, followed by a phone number

So what does RSVP mean? RSVP stands for a French phrase that means "Please reply". It is important to call whoever is hosting the party and let them know if we will or won't be able to attend. This allows the host to plan correctly for the party. The host has to know how much food to prepare, the number of party favors to make, how many chairs to have, and other important details. Once you have committed to go to a party, it is important and polite that you keep your commitment. It's also important that you RSVP very soon after you receive your invitation. This gives the host plenty of time to prepare adequately for the party. After you have responded to the invitation, it's time to mark your calendars and get ready to PARTY! It's going to be fun.

See you next time.

Activity
Have a discussion with your children on the importance of keeping our commitments, once we have committed to attending an event. The only time it is acceptable to cancel is for emergencies. Discuss what would qualify as an emergency. It would be rude to cancel your attendance because a better offer came along.

Day 45
Gift Giving

Now, for the fun part; if you're like me, you love buying presents for others. It usually requires several steps to buy someone a present. We start with thinking of the person we're buying for and trying to remember the things that they like to do and the things they are interested in. Usually we come up with a few options that we might be able to purchase for them, so now it's time to go to the store. It's important when shopping for others that we try our best to visualize (imagine) what that person would think of certain items. For instance, if you find a red sweater that you think is simply beautiful and you want to buy it for your Grandma, stop and think for a minute if you have ever seen her wear red. If you can't think of ever seeing her in red, then probably that's not one of her favorite colors. It's easy for us to buy things that we like, but we forget that we all have very different tastes. Similarly, if we're shopping for our friend and we see an army guy set that to us is simply awesome, ask yourself if you have ever known your friend to play with such things. Stopping for just a minute and visualizing who you're shopping for will help ensure that your gift will be more appreciated and enjoyed. Once we've found the perfect item, it's time to go and purchase the wrapping material (gift paper or gift bag, note card and ribbon). Finally it's time for the wrapping. This is not always easy but it's an important part of the gift giving process. If you went to buy a box of cereal and all the cereal in the store were in plain brown cardboard boxes with just the name of the cereal written on it, it would be hard to get excited about purchasing some cereal; likewise with presents. The more attractive the wrapping, the more exciting it is to unwrap. Whoo…finally we're done. That was a lot of work to just buy one present wasn't it? I hope they enjoy the present, don't you? See you next time.

Activity
This activity is so effective. Get a poster board and have your children list all the separate steps it takes to buy someone a present. You should be able to come up with around 10. For instance, one step is actually getting in the car and driving to the store. After listing the steps, estimate the time it took for each step. Add this up. When our children see the time, effort and money it takes to buy a single present, they are more likely to show their appreciation for the gift.

Day 46
Receiving Gifts

I hope that after we discussed gift giving in the previous lesson, we all have more appreciation for the time, effort and love that go into buying gifts for others. That sets up the discussion for today's lesson perfectly. Of course, we all love to receive gifts. It's exciting to open a present and wonder what could possibly be inside. Now that we have more respect for the gift giver, I hope that we will consider what we've learned as we receive and open our gifts. This means that a quick, quiet "thank you" and then quickly moving on to the next present, is not showing enough gratitude to the gift giver. We need to look at and examine our gift and express our pure delight in our gift. We need to look into the eyes of the gift giver and say, "Thank you so much, Grandpa, for the model kit. I can't wait for us to put it together and after we do, I'm going to put in on my desk where I can admire it." Do you see the difference between that kind of "thank you" and just a quick "thank you"? There is a difference and the gift giver will feel the difference. Sometimes we will receive a gift that we do not care for or do not particularly like. It is rude to ever express these feelings to the gift giver or to others. We do not have to lie; however, we can use tact to find things about the gift that are worth complimenting, for instance, "Oh Sarah, this is so unique. Thank you for your thoughtfulness. You always find the most interesting gifts." Remember to always consider the gift giver's feelings when opening presents, and enjoy all your presents. See you next time.

Activity
We're going to practice what to say when opening gifts. The teacher will use note cards and write, "You have opened a gift from…and it contains…What will your response be? Make it fun by placing cards in a paper bag and each person draws a card and responds. Get creative with those gift ideas.

Day 47
Arriving to the Party

One of the most important rules to remember when attending a party is to **ARRIVE ON TIME**. It is rude to arrive late to a party. The host has planned the time of the party for a reason and usually has the activities planned out on a time schedule. For instance, the host might have planned the first thirty minutes for welcoming and relaxing, the next thirty minutes for games, then eating, and the last thirty minutes for opening presents and giving party bags. By arriving on time, we honor the host and the plans they have made.

As we arrive to a birthday party, we ask the host where they would like us to put the present, and then we go find the birthday boy or girl and wish them a Happy Birthday and tell them how excited we are to be at their party.

If you're the host of the party, remember to introduce your guest to anyone they don't already know. It is the job of the host to make sure everyone has been introduced, so everyone feels welcomed and included.

Finally, just as arriving on time is important; it is also polite to leave on time. We never know what commitments the host has after the party, so make sure we do not linger past the scheduled time for the party to end. It's hard to leave when you're having so much fun, but we want to make sure we're invited back to the next party. See you next time.

Activity
Today, learn to wrap a present. Get all the supplies ready and use a big table to practice on. Also have fun creating ways to wrap a present that make it unique, like using paint, stickers, ribbons, glitter, etc. Award your children with, "most creative", "neatest", "fastest wrapper", "most cost effective", etc. Have fun!!!

Day 48
Birthday Boy or Girl, Center of Attention

This is an etiquette skill that often times, gets overlooked. You know how special it feels when it's your birthday. You want everyone to know, and you want people to make a "big deal" about it, especially your friends and family. Wanting special treatment one day out of 365 days in the year is not too much to ask, is it? Remembering how you want to feel on your birthday is a great way to help us know how to treat others on their birthday: very special. We want to help make the birthday boy or girl feel loved, valued and much appreciated. That's why, when we're attending a birthday party, we don't want to do things that draw attention to ourselves and away from the one we are honoring. Being too loud or too obnoxious would not be considered polite. Also, whispering or telling private stories that the honored boy or girl can't hear would also be considered rude. Just remember to help keep the focus on the birthday girl or boy so that they may have a wonderful birthday, and hopefully they will do the same when it's your turn to be honored. See you next time.

Activity
This can be great fun and the beginning of great family traditions. Discuss with your family different ideas of how you can honor the members of your family on their birthday. These are things that don't cost money, for instance, breakfast in bed, allowing them to sit in the front seat all day, having a special birthday plate and placemat to eat on (these can be made), doing the birthday boy or girl's chores for the day, etc.

Day 49
Participating at a Party

If you've ever planned and hosted a party, you know how important it is to you that everyone who attends has a really good time. It makes us feel good to know that our party was a big success and that everyone was glad they came. When someone plans a party, a lot of thought and effort goes into the planning. The host tries to think of games that everyone will like and activities that will be enjoyable. That's why we never want to complain about an activity, and we always want to participate. We would NEVER, NEVER, NEVER say, "This is boring," or "I'm bored." These two comments are extremely rude and would be very hurtful to the host or birthday girl or boy. We would also never say, "This isn't fun," or "Can we do something else?" Once again, these types of comments would not be polite. Make sure we participate in all the activities and games, even if we would rather not. By participating, we show appreciation for the effort the host has made in planning the activities. Watching the birthday girl or boy open their presents, is another important way to participate. The only time it is OK for you to decline participation in an activity at a party is if the activity makes you feel uncomfortable and uneasy. We NEVER lower our standards to participate in an activity. However, it's fun to try new things. You never know when a new activity will become your favorite sport or hobby. See you next time.

Activity
This is a great time to come up with fun creative ideas for games and activities for parties. Start a file that your family can add to as you learn about games and activities that sound like a lot of fun. You would be amazed how valuable this file will become on rainy days or when parties need a new direction. Speak to your children about how to handle situations at parties when the activity is not something they feel comfortable to participate in. Practicing these responses is an important way to help keep our children out of trouble and give them the confidence they need to make difficult decisions.

Day 50
Declining Party Foods

What happens when you're offered food at a party that you simply do not like? How do you handle it? Well, carefully. It isn't polite to ever announce that we don't particularly care for a food item. The best way to handle this kind of situation is one of two ways: you may simply say "no thank you" when offered the food item or, you may accept the item, but then leave it on your plate. Either way would be acceptable, so follow whichever way is more comfortable for you. This is usually a great time to use tact. For instance you could say, "Oh, no thank you, Mrs. Irvine. I don't care for any pizza right now, but I have my eye on that cupcake over there with the big red rose on it. It has my name written all over it." This would draw attention to what you are looking forward to instead of what you are declining. The host would feel complimented by your excitement over the cupcakes. Just remember to keep all your dislikes to yourself, but compliment all the things you enjoy. See you next time.

Activity
OK, definitely time to "role play". Get up and practice. Let your children pretend to be the host and the guest and practice different situations declining foods. The most important rule to remind them is that, "no one at the party should know what you dislike, no one". Have some laughs. The Host can "press" with questions and the guest has to remember the rule and do the best he/she can. Enjoy!!

Day 51
Thanking the Host

Well, you've reached the most important part of attending any party: thanking the host. I know all of you have probably been reminded by your parents hundreds of times to, "remember to say thank you". Am I right? I know I am, because I'm a mom, and I know how many times I've reminded my children. Because this is nothing new for you, I will only spend a moment on the subject. Nothing makes someone feel better, smile brighter and feel so loved as the feeling of appreciation. Isn't that what all of us want: to feel appreciated? At the end of a party or any event where the hosts have spent their valuable time, and often times, hard-earned money in arranging, planning, cooking, purchasing and hosting, they deserve a big, sincere "Thank you". "Thank you so much, Mr. and Mrs. Smith, for inviting me and hosting this wonderful party. I had such a good time. The food was delicious and the games were so much fun. I appreciate all you did to make it special." Wow, how wonderful and appreciated would a "thank you" like that make Mr. and Mrs. Smith feel. Think about it. See you next time.

Activity
Fun, fun, fun. Let's make some stationary, so you're ready for the next time you need to send a thank you card, such as after you've attended a party. Most computers have programs where you can personalize your own stationary. Try it and be creative. If you don't have access to a computer, you can purchase a pack of solid white or cream colored cards with envelopes at most craft stores. Design at least five cards. Have fun!!

Day 52
Sending Thank-You Cards

It's important and extremely polite to remember to send a thank you card when we receive a gift or an act of kindness. Remember when we talked about apologies and the importance of being sincere? Well the same principle applies to sending thank-you cards. We want our thank you to be sincere and from "the heart". An example of this might be:

Dear Michelle,

Thank you so much for coming to my birthday party. I always have more fun when you're around. I also want to thank you for the lovely picture frame you gave me. I can't wait to place a picture from my party in it. It will look great on my dresser. I hope all is well with you and your family.

Sincerely,
Robin

This thank you-note tells Michelle how much Robin appreciates her presence at the party and not only thanks her for the gift, but tells her how she will be using the gift. I'm sure Michelle will feel she made the right choice when she chose the picture frame, by the enthusiasm Robin expressed in the note. Be sincere and specific when you send someone a thank-you card. It doesn't have to be long. A text thank-you or an email thank-you is not acceptable however. Take the time to write and mail a note to recognize or acknowledge the effort that was made to purchase your gift. See you next time.

Activity
Make a "thank you" box. Get a shoebox and fill it with a variety of "thank you" notes. Place pens, envelopes and stamps in the box. Now you will always be ready to send "thank you" cards and will be more likely to send them in a timely manner. Keep your address book near your "thank you" shoebox. Decorating the shoebox is also really fun. Make sure you include your personalized stationary in your box. Enjoy!!!

Day 53
When to Send Cards

There are other reasons we should send a card to someone besides when we have received a gift. Cards are a great way to lift someone's spirit and to let them know we are thinking of them. Here are some reasons we might want to send someone a card:

1. New Address—we've moved—let all your friends and family know your new address, so the next time they need to send you something, they already have your new address

2. Special Holidays—remembering holidays that you know are special to your friends or family are a great reason to send a card honoring that holiday

3. Congratulations—it's fun to congratulate someone on important accomplishments like school graduation, marriage, birth of baby, baptism, new job, new house, etc.

4. Wedding Anniversary—this sends a great message of respect and admiration to those who have made their marriage work.

5. Sympathy—people who are going through trials in their life
appreciate it when others send cards of encouragement and sympathy.
It's a great idea to keep blank stationary and stamps on your desk so that sending a card to someone is more convenient. Keep your address book accurate and have fun sending cards. See you next time.

Activity
Write and send a card to someone. Have your children think of someone who has given them a gift or someone who has been kind to them and send them a thank you card…or think of someone who needs a sympathy card or congratulation's card. Keep on the "look out" for cards on sale. "Stock up" when you can and add these cards to your shoebox. There are also great "MINI Filing" containers that are great for organizing cards.

Day 54
Wedding Anniversary Gifts

A wedding anniversary is an exciting occasion to honor those we love who have achieved "marriage milestones". Whether it's your mom and dad, grandma and grandpa or simply friends, buying a wedding anniversary gift can actually be fun when you cherish an old tradition of certain gifts for certain years. Basically it works like this; depending on which anniversary it is, there are certain kinds of gifts you buy. Th tradition is only for certain milestones which are the following:

1 year—Paper (like stationary)

5 year—Wood (like wooden salad bowls or a wooden picture frame)

10 year—Tin (like a tin canister or a tin wall hanging)

15 year—Crystal (like a crystal bowl or crystal candle holders)

20 year—China (like a piece for their china collection)

25 year—Silver (like a silver platter or sterling silverware)

50 year—Gold (anything gold; jewelry, serving spoon, etc.)

75 year—Diamond (Diamonds!!!!!!)

Keep this list around your house, and I promise that there will be occasions in your life when it will come in handy, even when you're shopping for your spouse someday. I love SHOPPING!!!! See you next time.

Activity
Make an anniversary date list. List the major anniversary milestones of your parents, grandparents and anyone else you want to remember. Go ahead and write the dates of the milestones so you don't have to keep adding in your head each year. These are usually fun gifts to shop for because you have a real purpose in your gift buying. You will really gladden the heart of those you remember with such a thoughtful gesture.

Day 55
Gifts for the Host

This is an etiquette consideration that is not necessary, but is very thoughtful and can be a lot of fun. Of course, we know that when we go to a birthday party, we usually take a gift unless the host has requested "no gifts". However, there are other times when it is appropriate to take a gift to a host. These gifts are simple gestures that show our gratitude for the host and his/her accommodations. For instance, if you're going to stay at your aunt's house for the weekend, it would be polite to take her a fresh loaf of bread or perhaps a candle (something small but thoughtful). Food is usually a gift that is well received because it doesn't make the host feel like you spent too much money, yet it shows you were thinking of her and you appreciate her hospitality. Likewise, when you go to someone's house for a dinner party, a fun bottle of seltzer or maybe a collection of chocolates would be a simple, yet thoughtful, gift. This is not something you should spend a lot of money on. Less than $10.00 is perfectly appropriate. Have fun with this etiquette consideration. It's fun to try to think of a small gift that would be unique for your friend or relative, and definitely starts your visit out on the "right foot".

Activity
Plan ahead! Planning ahead can sure make life easier. With your family, think of whose houses you are invited to for dinner and overnight visits for the whole family. Then, brainstorm and come up with some great, inexpensive ideas that you could take as a host gift to those individuals. If you can, go ahead and acquire needed supplies, so the next time your family visits, you are prepared to take the host a special gift. Kids really get excited about gift giving when they are involved in the planning, purchases and giving stages. Enjoy!!!

Day 56
Conversations

Believe it or not, good conversations take skills and practice. There are actual skills that we can acquire to help us become better a conversationalist. You may be asking yourself, "Why do I need to be a good conversationalist?" Well, I'll tell you. When you talk to someone, do you want to be understood? Do you want people to hear you? Do you think it's important to understand and hear what other people are saying? Do you think that sometimes people misunderstand each other, and that this can cause hurt feelings and confusion? The answer to all of these questions is "yes". So here are some skills that we need to practice and perfect, so that these problems do not occur in our conversations. First, make eye contact and keep eye contact with the person you are communicating with. This simple act lets the other person know that you are interested in what they are saying and you are engaged (involved) in the conversation. When we aren't looking into the eyes of the one who is speaking, the speaker wonders whether or not we are truly listening. This can be very frustrating for the speaker, and it is not very respectful to them, either. Next, we need to make sure we are listening to their words. This means we can't be thinking of other things when we're trying to listen. Another needed skill, is to stay on the subject. When someone is trying to talk to us about our weekend plans, for example, it is not the time to start talking about what we ate for dinner last night. Try to stay on the subject until both parties are satisfied that the conversation has been completed. Practice, practice, practice. See you next time.

Activity
First, have two people come to the front. One person starts telling the other person what they did last weekend. Whisper to the "listening person" to occasionally look at the person speaking but mostly look away towards other things. Tell the speaker he/she must speak for one minute. Time them. After this experiment, ask the speaker to describe what this experience was like. Words like frustrating, irritating and rude will probably come to mind. Use this experiment to further the discussion.

Day 57
Balance in Conversations

No, we're not done with conversations. I'll bet you didn't know that there were so many skills involved in speaking to others. I know it might sound kind of boring (learning how to be a great communicator and conversationalist), but if you could, just trust me when I tell you that excelling at these skills will benefit your life in every way you can imagine. Most problems in the family, with our co-workers, in our churches, and everywhere else, usually begin from a lack of communication skills. So let's continue to improve. Have you ever been in a conversation with someone, and you can't seem to get two words in because the person you're speaking with won't be quiet long enough for you to enter the conversation? Yeah, me too. Instead of getting upset about it, let's just learn from it. There needs to be balance in our conversations. We need to make sure we give others equal amounts of "speaking time". We also need to be careful that our conversation is not all about us. I call it the "me, myself and I conversation". That's when someone just can't quite quit talking about themselves. Some of us refer to it as bragging or boasting. Regardless of what we call it, I think we all know what it means. A good way to make sure we don't get into this habit is take turns asking and telling in your conversations. If you tell someone about your pet, after you're done speaking, ask about their pet. If you talk about your family, in turn, ask about theirs. This is a great way to keep the conversation in good balance: equal amounts of talking and listening. Just remember, talk and ask. Practice. See you next time.

Activity
Get up and practice. Use a timer to time the children as they talk. Divide the children up into pairs. Give them a subject matter, like their favorite vacation, and then tell them they have 2 minutes to tell their partner about their vacation. When the timer goes off, the other person will have the same amount of time to describe. Give them 2 or 3 topics to discuss, so they can get a good feel for how the flow of the conversation goes. This will really help them think about taking turns, the next time their in a conversation. Have Fun!

Day 58
Think Before You Speak

Sometimes, we speak before we think about what we are saying. I'm sure that if you're like me, you have said something and then after you said it, you thought, "Why on earth did I ever say that? What was I thinking?" Well, the answer is, we weren't thinking. That's the problem. Once again, we learn from our mistakes. If we learn from our mistakes, they're not really just mistakes, but stepping stones that we can use to cross the valley of life. The best advice I can give is this: think about what kind of effect your words could have on others, before you speak them. For instance, one time I was at a baby shower and I was in charge of taking the pictures. There was a young woman there wearing a blouse that looked to me like a maternity top (clothes for pregnant women). So I called out to her and the "real" pregnant lady saying, "Let's get a picture of the two 'mothers to be'." Well, the young woman was not pregnant. I was horrified. I learned a valuable lesson that day, which is never, never, never assume someone is pregnant. The point is to make sure we know what we're talking about before we speak. Now, I try to ask myself this question before I speak "Could these words cause hurt or misunderstanding to those who hear them?" If so, I think carefully before I let the words leave my lips. Be careful with your words, they can have a long-lasting impact on others. See you next time.

Activity
This is a good time to have the children reflect on past experiences. Ask the children to write down a time when they spoke words they wish they could take back. After writing about the wrong words spoken, have the children write down what would have been better words to speak. If everyone is feeling courageous, allow the children to give their new words to whomever they were meant for. Usually a sincere apology verbalized upon delivery of the new words, is very appropriate. (Don't force the kids to deliver these words, only encourage.

Day 59
Never Reveal Confidences

Another common and more serious error of judgment is repeating "confidences" (information someone has told you in private). This is so important, I can't stress it enough. When someone confides in you, please keep that information to yourself. Unless you feel that keeping that confidence could possibly jeopardize the safety of that person or someone else, you should never "pass along" that information to others. Be trustworthy, keep your word. Even if someone doesn't actually say, "please don't tell anyone", you can assume that it is expected, unless the person gives you permission to tell others. Remember, we are trying to improve our integrity, which is directly affected by our ability to earn the trust of others. Probably one of the most hurtful things between close friends and family occurs when confidences are revealed by those we trust. When this happens, we feel betrayed and usually this betrayal is a difficult thing for us to forget and move past. Think about this before you pass on information. It could save a friendship, or your relationship with family members. Now, there is an important exception to this consideration. When you are a child, there should be no secrets from your parents. Your parents are responsible for your well-being, as well as that of other children, and telling your parents does not count in revealing confidences. You never have to fear being untrustworthy when you reveal confidences to your parents. See you next time.

Activity
Now is an important time to talk to your children about good secrets and bad secrets. A good secret is not telling your mom what her birthday present is. Bad secrets are information that would cause hurt, pain or sorrow to others. We must encourage our children that it is not safe to keep secrets from their parents. Usually, children keep secrets because they are scared of our reactions. It is important to ensure our children that we will remain calm and we will work through issues with love, understanding and forgiveness. Although accountability will be considered, it will be fair and considered with love. This should be an ongoing conversation with our children. Good Luck!

Day 60
Be Positive

When we're speaking to others, we have to consider whom we're speaking with. When we're speaking with casual acquaintances (friends or associates with whom we do not have especially close relationships), it is polite to keep our conversation light and upbeat. This means that we don't linger (spend too long), speaking of ills, misfortunes or other unpleasantness. I used to know a person who went around frowning all the time. Whenever I would say hello and ask her how she was doing, she would immediately begin describing all her misfortunes and all the hardships in her life. After I spoke with her, I was always sad or in a more somber mood. This continued and eventually I realized that this person never had anything positive to say, which caused me to not want to engage in conversation with her. That might sound like I didn't care about her misfortune, which was not true. I did care, and I tried to help her as much as I could. But, if all we ever do is complain and focus on all the bad in our lives, it causes others to tend to stay away. Who wants to be "dragged down" every time they see someone? I soon realized that I wanted to make sure I wasn't someone who other people dreaded to run into. I wanted to make sure that others were "lifted" when they left a conversation with me. This is not to say I am perfect at this skill or that I never complain. I wish I didn't, but I know I still do. Let's just try to remember to be positive, especially with casual acquaintances so we can help them be lifted instead of lowered. I'll keep trying to improve, as well. See you next time.

Activity
Once again, further discussion on this topic would be a great idea. We don't want our children to be afraid to tell someone when they are sad, mad or upset about something; however, we need to make sure our children understand the difference between casual acquaintances and those they can confide in. Here's a great challenge for the whole family: Choose a day in the coming week for the entire family to agree that nothing negative is going to be said ALL DAY LONG. Whoo, this is hard. I mean nothing!!! It's important that everyone does this together to help hold each other accountable. At the end of the day, sit down and let everyone describe their feelings about the experiment. Have Fun!!!

Day 61
Keep It Interesting

This is kind of a funny consideration for me because someone I know has a slight problem with this. However I would never tell him because I wouldn't want to hurt his feelings. See if this sounds familiar. You know someone, it might even be you, who has had an experience. Let's say the experience was what happened to you in the grocery store line last night. Well, you want to tell about it. Oh, goody…a story. You start telling the story and the details are very specific. The story goes…..and goes…..and goes….. and goes….. Those listening start to wonder how an incident that probably only lasted 5-10 seconds, could take so long to tell. Sometimes, we get a little "carried away" with the details of a story. Just because something is very interesting to you, does not mean that it is just as interesting to everyone else. Keep this is mind when telling a story. We don't want to bore others with too many details. It's also polite to try not to repeat stories. Sometimes if you're not sure if you've already told someone a story, ask them, "Have I told you what happened to my dog last week at the vet?" If they say, "Yes, you did", you can stop and not bore them with a repeated story. This is a polite consideration that all of us appreciate. It's hard to hear a story more than once and try to act enthusiastic about it. One last bit of advice: don't pretend to know more about something than you really do. It's a good way to look pretty silly. Sometimes people like to try to impress others by acting like they know a lot. This can really "backfire" if you try to speak on a subject you're not really familiar with. It's best to just say, "I haven't had a lot of experience with that". It's the smartest thing you can say sometimes. See you next time.

Day 62
Conversation "No-No's"

Have you ever witnessed two people arguing in public? This is extremely rude. We never, never argue or disagree in public unless we are on a debate team. There are some conversations that are only appropriate in private, and disagreements are one of them. Hopefully, even when we disagree, we are respectful to the one we are disagreeing with. This would mean that we do not use critical language, we do not raise our voice, we listen to their opinion without interrupting, and we accept that it is not our job to force everyone to agree with us. People are different. We have different opinions. We value things differently. It's what makes the "world go round". It is acceptable to have a difference of opinion with another. We must, however, always be considerate of others' feelings, and that includes individuals who do not want their afternoon to be interrupted by a loud disagreement. This would not be pleasant or polite.

A second consideration we must remember is that it is not polite to speak of financial matters in public. It is not polite to ask someone how much something cost, or how much their salary is, or other such financial questions. These matters are very personal and should be discussed only in private conversations. Please consider this, because this topic often makes a person uncomfortable, which is the opposite of proper etiquette. Be kind, and remember these considerations. See you next time.

Activity
Take your children one by one and place them in front of a wall. Instruct them to argue with the wall. Be serious, as this is a serious experiment (well sort of). Tell them to yell, scream, do whatever, but you want to hear an argument. Hopefully, they will have trouble with this experiment. The point to make afterward is that it is absolutely impossible to have an argument with a wall. In fact, it is impossible to have an argument with someone who is not willing to argue back. Hopefully, they will consider this the next time someone tries to have an argument with them. Enjoy!

Day 63
Interrupting

I'm sure that most of us have been taught that interrupting someone while they're speaking with someone else is not polite. Although this is true, I've found that there are several forms of impolite interrupting that sometimes have not been considered. For instance, when two adults are speaking to one another, it is not polite to go and stand right beside them to wait for your opportunity to speak. You must consider that unless you've been invited to join the conversation, the conversation is private. This means that along with not interrupting, we must not "listen in" on a conversation that we are not a part of. Standing so close that you can hear the conversation is a type of interrupting and could also be considered eavesdropping (listening to a conversation between two others without being invited to do so). The appropriate thing to do would be to stand at a distance where you cannot hear the conversation, but close enough that, when you see a pause in the conversation, you may say something like, "Excuse me Mom, but when you have a minute, I need to ask you something." This way you have made it known that you need to talk to Mom, but you have kept an appropriate distance so as not to disturb the conversation. Another form of interrupting is simply "butting in" right in the middle of someone else's sentence. This is very frustrating to the person who was interrupted, because it causes them to loose their "train of thought", and sometimes they never get it back. This happens to me all the time. Be careful not to interrupt in any way. If we are always considerate of others, we will not have a problem with this impolite behavior. See you next time.

Activity
Role Playing Time. Have one child stand and tell him/her to share something with the rest of the students that was really important to them, such as when they won their ballgame, or when they hiked a big mountain, etc. Whisper to someone else to interrupt the story teller 2 or 3 times during the story. The story teller should try to continue their story where they left off at the end of each interruption. Go for a couple of minutes and then let the children discuss their feelings during the experiment.

Day 64
Entering Group Conversation

What do you do when you want to join a group already having a conversation? I'm sure you've walked into a room where a group of friends are sitting around a table in conversation, and you would like to join them. What is the appropriate and polite way to join them? Well, first approach the group without drawing too much attention to yourself, so that you don't distract the others from the conversation already in progress. Next, make eye contact with those whom you know and give them a smile. This is an unspoken "hello". Hopefully, as soon as a person stops talking, someone will say, "Hi Barrett. It's great to see you here. Has everyone met Barrett? We were just discussing the new basketball court on the playground." Then Barrett would join in the discussion about the basketball court. It would not be polite for Barrett to join the group and immediately start talking about something unrelated to the subject being discussed, like, "Hey you guys. You are never going to believe what just happened. I was walking down the hall and a giant banana started chasing me. It was so freaky." We want to join in on conversation without detracting from it, but "adding" to it. This is polite and courteous behavior. Remember, if you're in the group and someone approaches, be the one to smile and make eye contact with them and then wait for the right opportunity (a break in the conversation) to welcome them and introduce the "joiner" to everyone who doesn't know him/her. This way everyone always feels welcome. See you next time.

Activity
This is a great group role playing opportunity. Have the children form a circle and begin a conversation of their choice. Allow another child to approach the group and practice their etiquette as they say "hello", and wait for the appropriate time to enter the conversation. Also, watch the group and make sure someone has invited in the new comer and introduced him/her to everyone else and to the conversation at the appropriate time. Enjoy!

Day 65
Exiting Conversation

What do you do when you're ready to leave a conversation? Well, as always, we want to consider the other person's feelings. What if you were talking to your best friend and telling him/her about the latest level of Spiderman that you just beat on Nintendo DS, which took you three hours by the way. Then, all of a sudden in the middle of your sentence, your friend says, "Luke, I need to run and look at my eyes in the mirror and make sure they're still the same color as they were yesterday. See ya." So how do you think you would feel? Well first, I hope you're investigating why this guy is your best friend, but second, your feelings would probably be hurt. It wasn't an appropriate time for your friend to exit the conversation, and he didn't use polite manners to do so. We need to wait for an appropriate break in the conversation, when we believe that the person has been able to express his/her thoughts thoroughly. Then we can say something like, "Sterling, it has been so good to get to talk to you. You've been doing some exciting things with your life. I need to run so I can grab some lunch, but I hope it's not too long before we can see each other again. Take care, and I hope I see you soon." This would show that we value our friend Sterling and have enjoyed talking to him. We both leave the conversation feeling satisfied and uplifted. Things that send unspoken messages of boredom that should always be avoided in conversations are fidgeting, yawning, rolling your eyes, switching from foot to foot, looking away, texting, picking your nails, twisting your hair around your fingers and tapping your fingers or your feet. We never want to do something to cause another person hurt or pain. Enjoy your conversations, even if it's not about your favorite subject. It's not going to kill you to listen for twenty minutes about the latest makes and models of trucks; if so, I would be dead. I have had to listen to this type of conversation many times from my husband. See you next time.

Activity
Play "Story Line". One person says most of a sentence about something fictional they did, for instance, "We were walking down a street in New York City when all of a sudden this man approached us and asked us if…" Then the next person finishes the sentence and starts a new sentence. It continues around the room at least twice. There's no real teaching moment here. Just have fun using your imagination.

Day 66
Slamming Doors

Instead of discussing this impolite behavior known as "slamming the door", I turn to a poem I had my son memorize quite some time ago. You'll be glad that I'm not your mother after you read this poem. Some of you, I'm quite sure, you are familiar with it:

Rebecca, Who Slammed Doors for Fun and Perished Miserably
By Hilaire Belloc

A trick that everyone abhors in little girls is slamming doors.
A wealthy banker's little daughter who lived in Palace Green, Bayswater
(By name Rebecca Offendort), was given to this Furious Sport.

She would deliberately go and slam the door like Billy-Ho!
To make her Uncle Jacob start. She was not actually bad at heart,
But only rather rude and wild: She was an aggravating child…

It happened that a marble bust of Abraham was standing just
Above the door this little lamb had carefully prepared to slam,
And down it came! It knocked her flat!
It laid her out! She looked like that.

Her funeral sermon (which was long and followed by a sacred song)
Mentioned her virtues, it is true, but dwelt upon her vices too,
And showed the dreadful end of one who goes and slams the door for fun.

The children who were brought to hear the awful tale from far and near
Were much impressed, and inly swore they never more would slam the door.
--As often they had done before.

Need I say more? See you next time.

Day 67
Filtering Our Conversation

Depending on who we are with, we sometimes talk about certain subjects and avoid others. This is simply another way we consider the feelings of others. For instance, if we're visiting someone who is not feeling well and unable to get outside at the present time, it would not be polite to engage in a conversation about what a beautiful day it is outside and why it's the perfect day to be outside, enjoying the weather. Or if you're speaking to an elderly person, it would not be polite to speak of how much you dread getting older and losing the ability to care for yourself. Yet another example would be speaking to someone who is in a wheelchair about how fast you can run. Sometimes, we say these things without thinking, but we need to be careful, so that we don't appear insensitive to the difficulties of others. Try to find things you have in common with those you communicate with, so that the conversation can be uplifting to both of you. We've gone over many communication skills. I hope that you and your family enjoy increasing your skills, and that pretty soon you will see and feel the benefit of great communication skills. It takes time, so don't get discouraged. Work on one thing at a time, and before you know it, it will feel natural. Good luck, and I'll see you next time.

Activity
It's really time to put to use all our newly formed communication etiquette skills. Plan a time this week that your whole family can go to a nursing home to visit the elderly. When we go, we simply walk into a room and ask, "Would you care for any company?" If they do, sit down and enjoy talking to your new friend. I know this can be intimidating; be strong, be courageous…the elderly usually love to have young visitors.

Day 68
Telephone Manners

I love it when my friends call, don't you? Talking to friends and family on the phone can be fun, and it's a great way to stay connected with those we care about. There are a few considerations when answering and talking on the phone. Have you ever called someone and asked to speak to them and the person who answered the phone all of a sudden screams out, "Jennifer, you're friend who wears those funny shoes is on the phone….Jennnifferrr!!!" Well, now that you've lost hearing in one ear, you probably are thinking, "That wasn't very polite." It wasn't polite. Yelling into the phone is never polite and can actually cause discomfort to the other person. When someone calls, let's remember a few polite considerations, so that everyone feels respected and at ease. The first thing we want to do when answering the phone is say a polite greeting
like, "Hello" or "Good Morning." When the person asks to speak to someone, we politely say, "Sure, one moment please. May I ask who is calling?" Then we quietly and quickly take the phone to that person with our hand over the receiver so the caller doesn't hear all the commotion of our home. We then can hand over the phone and identify who is calling: "Mom, it's your friend Mrs. Roads." If the person they ask for is not home, we have a few options. We may ask them to call back a little later, or we may write down their information and then make sure we communicate that information accurately and in a timely manner. It's important to be very responsible when taking caller information. We never know how important a message is, so treat each one with the utmost care. Lastly, proper etiquette means that we don't call others after 9:00pm or before 8:00am. We must respect people's sleep. See you next time.

Activity
Today get a pad of paper and a pen and place them beside every phone in your house. Now you will be prepared to take messages accurately for your family. Discuss with your family the way messages are to be taken in your home.

Day 69
Telephone Safety

Safety is very important when talking on the telephone. The most important rule that we can remember is this: Never give out personal information (name, address, other family members' names, etc.) to strangers over the phone. Sometimes a caller may ask for someone who does not reside at your home. In this case you simply say, "I'm sorry, you must have the wrong number." Then you hang up. If the caller tries to ask personal questions like, "Well, who am I speaking to?" you simply hang up. If you are uncomfortable in any way when speaking to a caller, hand the phone to your parents, or hang up. Talk to your parents about how to handle phone calls whenever you are home alone. Some parents do not like for their children to answer the phone when they are home alone, while others allow it. It is never a good idea for a child to tell a caller that he/she is home alone.

This is an uncomfortable topic to talk about, but it is important that you and your family discuss these phone safety rules, and that everyone is clear on how to handle them. When you don't feel safe, polite behavior is not a priority. Safety is always the most important thing. See you next time.

Activity
Discuss with your children how to handle phone calls when they are home alone. Make an emergency contact list with names of family or friends who are close, of emergency services, etc. and place by each phone. During emergencies, often people can get overwhelmed and forget phone numbers and names, so that's why it's important to have all that information by the phone ready for use.

Day 70
Good Behavior When Others Are Using The Phone

Now, I know that all of you can tell me several rules that fall under this category. But why do we sometimes have trouble following them? I'm sure that most of you are very respectful to those talking on the phone in your presence. This is a great form of proper etiquette. Have you ever considered why we should use our manners when someone else is talking on the phone? The truth is, we never know exactly what is being discussed on the phone between two people. The person at the other end of the phone could be speaking of something very important, like the loss of a job or the birth of a baby, or something extremely sad, like the death of a loved one. Out of respect for both the other caller and the person to whom they are speaking, we should try to be very quiet when others are on the phone and even give them privacy when we can. It is not polite to eavesdrop on others' conversations, as we discussed earlier. If you ever pick up the phone and someone else is using it, quietly hang the phone up. It is not polite to interrupt someone on the phone, unless it is an absolute emergency. Your "lego" truck being eaten by the dog is not an emergency; a tragedy, yes, but emergency, no. Try not to make irritating noises or cause any other disruption that would distract the callers from their conversation. This consideration is one that will benefit you, as others will, in turn, be respectful of you when you are on the phone. See you next time.

Activity
Now is a good time to discuss with your class what is considered an emergency and what is not. Sometimes it is helpful to invent a "secret signal" that your family can use to express the need to communicate. For instance, touching your nose or touching the other person's hand. Really, anything that could be done discreetly would work.
Have fun!

Day 71
Cell Phone Etiquette

Some of you may be a little young for a cell phone, but it is never too early to learn proper etiquette for cell phone use so when you do get your first cell phone, you will be prepared to use it properly. Here is a great list of etiquette considerations to ponder for cell phone usage:

1. Don't speak too loudly. Others present do not wish to hear the details of your conversation, so speak softly when in public, or retreat to a place of privacy.

2. Be careful that the conversation is not inappropriate for "public ears".

3. Don't answer your phone if you are in the middle of a conversation with someone else. This is simply interrupting, which is not proper etiquette.

4. Do not check phone messages at the movie theater. This distracts others present.

5. Absolutely do not text while driving. This could cost a life.

6. Do not text while you are speaking with someone else. This is the same as trying to have two conversations with two different people about two different subjects at the same time. This is rude and shows a lack of respect for both conversations.

7. Do not text "small talk". It's OK to text someone specific information, like what time a movie starts, or what time you need to be picked up. But if you want to see how someone is doing, have the courtesy to pick up the phone and call them so you can speak to them personally. It means a lot more.

8. Try not to have loud, annoying ring tones.

9. Keep cell phones turned off during live performances.

10. Location, location, location—there are several places where it is simply inappropriate to accept a call on your cell phone; for instance, the library, a doctor's office, in a check-out or order line. Just consider those around you before you take your next cell phone call, and be sure it is not going to distract others or be a nuisance to those around you.

Activity
Discuss!!!!

Day 72
Text Messaging

I know we talked a little about texting in the previous section, but I feel we need to spend a little more time discussing it. Number one, it has become an absolute craze for a lot of people, especially young people. I went to the movies not too long ago, and in front of me sat a family. Throughout the entire movie, their daughter was texting. Texting while others are trying to have some family time can send a message of disengagement (present in body but not in mind), and could cause hurt feelings among other family members. I thought it was kind of sad that this girl's parents were trying to have some family time with her; yet she was really not there. When we text while spending time with others, we are sending a message to those we're with: that we would rather be in communication with someone else than to be here with them. That doesn't go along with what we know about etiquette, does it? Remember the goal for good etiquette is to help make others feel comfortable and valued. It's OK to accept an important text on a rare occasion, by asking the person you're with, "Do you mind if I quickly respond to this text to clear up some information?" Then, put your phone away and resume your communication with those you're with. Be careful not to waste too many minutes or hours in the day texting.

Someone who possesses the skills of etiquette, uses moderation in all things, never wasting time that could be used more wisely in the pursuit of greatness. Things to consider. See you next time.

Activity
This is a topic that just simply needs to be discussed with empathy in mind. Allow your children to express their opinion without fear of judgment. I have found that the best way to get people to understand why it's rude to text while you're in the presence of others is to role play this scenario. Have three children sit side by side and pretend they are riding in a car. Tell the three children to begin a discussion about their favorite movie. Secretly, tell two of the three to occasionally whisper something to each other, leaving the third person out. After watching this for a few minutes, have the children describe their feelings about this experience. Hopefully they will see the relationship between texting and whispering.
Have fun discussing and learning.

Day 73
Social Networking Sites

Once again, some of you may be too young for using social networking sites. Social networking sites are "chat rooms": Facebook, MySpace and other types of websites. Extreme caution should be used when visiting these types of websites. As with the telephone, we never want to give out personal information via the internet, even if you think you know or can trust the person you are giving the information to. Private information should only be given in person to those you know and trust. Here is another voice of caution regarding these sites: please, never discuss matters that should only be discussed in private. Although we may believe that a conversation is only going to be between us and the person we trust, sometimes conversations are distributed to others, and can cause embarrassment and even anger. The rule is this: unless you want the whole world to hear or read your words, never send them via the internet. Also, we never want to send unkind messages that include teasing, bullying, gossiping or spreading rumors in any way via the internet. This is dangerous and inappropriate and should never be tolerated. Also, never put photos on the internet that you would not want the whole world, including your parents, to see. Pictures constantly get downloaded and sent to individuals who were never intended to see them. Be cautious and wise when using social networking sites. Honor your "house rules" and let your parents know if you ever feel uncomfortable or uneasy about people you communicate with via the internet. See you next time.

Activity
Make sure your children understand the rules for visiting social networking sites. There are many stories in the news of bullying, blackmailing and other forms of intimidation via the web. I encourage all parents to familiarize yourselves with these forms of communication, so that you may be more diligent in protecting your child. We must teach our children about the dangers on the web. Not talking about it does not work. Sit down with your children and make sure everyone understands the "house rules" and makes a commitment to abide by those rules.

Day 74
Good Hygiene

I bet you didn't consider hygiene (bodily cleanliness and appearance), as a part of proper etiquette. Well it is. I want you to look at the images below and think about what each picture tells you about the person. Do you think you could make a few guesses about what each person likes to do, or what is important to them? Or maybe you could guess where they are going. I bet you can, and you would probably be right. The way we dress and the way we keep our appearance plays a vital (important) role in the way in which people form opinions about us. I'm not speaking of how expensive your shoes are or whether or not you're wearing a "name brand" dress; I'm speaking of your hygiene, which covers several different areas. Let's imagine you are invited to go with your grandparents to a play at the local theater Friday night. They come to pick you up and you are dressed in dirty blue jeans with a t-shirt that has holes in the sleeves, where you like to stick your pencil. Your hair is a mess, and you're wearing flip-flops. How do you think your grandparents would respond? What message do you think you would be sending them? Perhaps they would feel like you didn't really care about the play or about spending time with them. We must realize that our appearance sends lots of messages, whether we realize it or not. Yes, we're told to not judge a book by its cover, but in reality, our first impression of people is usually greatly influenced by the way someone appears. Think about it, and we'll talk about the details in the next few sections. See you next time.

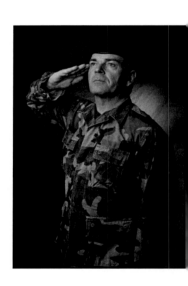

Day 75
Bodily Cleanliness

OK, go ahead and laugh if you want to. We should already know these things, but let's just make sure, OK? Keeping ourselves neat and clean influences the way we are perceived (judged) and accepted by others. It's a distasteful subject, however; have you ever tried to talk to someone who had bad body odor? It's not very easy to communicate and stay thoughtful during a conversation when you have to hold your breath between each sentence. This is something we need to be aware of and check for from time to time. As you know, keeping yourselves clean is the first step but there are different hygiene items such as deodorants, body sprays and perfumes that can help keep body odor at bay. Keeping our hair clean and neat is also important and leads to a healthier scalp and hair. Clean hands are another important part of bodily hygiene. Have you ever started to shake hands with someone, but then you noticed that their hands were so dirty that you would rather not touch them? This can be awkward. Keeping your hands clean helps those around you feel more comfortable and helps keep germs from spreading. Fingernails need to be kept clean and trimmed as well, since fingernails are a common gathering place for germs and bacteria. We never, never take care of bodily hygiene in public. This is extremely rude. This would include trimming or picking toenails, filing or polishing nails, combing or brushing hair, etc. These activities should be performed in private and in the appropriate places. See you next time.

Activity
Sometimes, as leaders and parents, we just assume that our children know certain things. Hygiene is not one of those things we want to take for granted. This is a great time to pull out hygiene items and explain the purpose for each of them. Take this time to allow your children to practice trimming their nails. Demonstrate the proper way to wash hands after using the restroom or before eating (warm water and soap for 20 seconds). Talk about the risk for head lice. Enjoy!!

Day 76
Clothes

We all have different tastes in clothes, and if you're like me, you believe that our clothes help us express our personalities. This is what's wonderful about clothes. I love to observe the different ways people dress, because I admire the creativeness expressed in clothes. Although we can all be different, one way we all need to be the same is by keeping our clothes clean and well cared for. Proper care of clothes includes washing them, folding or hanging them so that they're not wrinkled, and repairing tears and holes when we can. By doing these things, we help our clothes last a lot longer and show respect for those who purchased our clothes. We need to be thoughtful of others when it comes to the words and pictures on our clothes. Yes, we have freedom of expression in this great country; however that does not mean we can't be sensitive to the values of those around us, especially when children are present. Dressing modestly is another way we can be respectful and value the standards of those around us. If our clothes draw too much attention to us, we are distracting others or disrupting the events which we attend. Our clothes should not cause discomfort or uneasiness in any form to those we're with. Remember our definition for proper etiquette: to help make others comfortable and feel at ease. Lastly, we should dress according to the event or the people you are visiting. For instance, if we're going out with Grandpa and Grandma, and Grandpa and Grandma always "dress up," then we should "dress up," as well. If we're going to a rodeo, then jeans and a t-shirt would probably be fine. Just respect the event or those you're with by being thoughtful in your dress and appearance. See you next time.

Activity
Now is a great time to teach your children how to properly wash and care for their clothes. Begin by teaching the children how to separate clothes according to color or type. Then teach them how to set your washing machine to the correct temperature and spin cycle. Go through all the steps, allowing the children to do it with your supervision. Next, grab a couple of clothes items and teach your children how to iron. This, of course, would be for older children. Smaller children can learn to fold and put away their clothes. Then, practice, practice, practice.

Day 77
No "Dragon Breath"

Keeping our mouth clean and fresh is a great way to ensure we do not run off any potential friends. It's very difficult to talk to someone who has what we like to call "dragon breath" (no offense). We always want to brush our teeth, ideally, after every meal, but, realistically, at least twice each day. It's still a good idea if you can't brush your teeth, to at least get to a mirror after you eat and flash a smile to make sure you don't have left-over lunch between your teeth: not very attractive. Also, keeping breath mints handy is a great way to make sure your breath stays fresh. Remembering to consider how those around us feel, is why we try to keep our mouth clean. Overlooking this etiquette consideration could potentially cost you a job interview or an important relationship (like a future spouse). Good luck keeping those "pearly whites" sparkling and that breath "minty fresh". See you next time.

Activity
This is a great time to review the proper method for brushing and caring for our teeth. There are iodine tests that are fun to use so that your children can see all the plaque on their teeth. Review flossing, and, if possible, find a 2 minute timer that your children can use to make sure they are brushing long enough. Examine everyone's toothbrush and make sure they are in good condition.
Enjoy!

Day 78
Teasing

In the next several lessons, we will discuss some pretty serious subjects. I wish we didn't even have to discuss them; however, I want to ensure that everyone has considered the consequences of different types of behavior that are very unbecoming (unattractive) to those who practice proper etiquette. First, let's talk about teasing. Teasing means to annoy or torment someone else. I realize that there are different forms of teasing. Sometimes we playfully tease those we love with no intentional to harm. Although, such teasing is usually innocent in nature, we always run the risk that the person being teased, may be hurt. It's a very "tight rope" we walk between playful teasing and hurtful teasing. I try not to do either, because I do not think it's worth the risk of possibly hurting someone's feelings, even when I don't mean to. The other form of teasing is purposeful, and involves intentional hurting or embarrassing someone else. When people say things that they know will upset, anger, or embarrass another human being, they are engaging in rude behavior, which is the opposite of proper etiquette (making others feel good). Sometimes people tease those who look different from them, speak differently, or believe differently. No matter what, teasing others is a cowardly act and we should make sure we never participate in any kind of teasing, which includes joining in the laughter when someone else is being teased. One of the best ways to "fight off" teasing is to either ignore the person or laugh at yourself. Regardless of which way you choose, when you react in these ways, you have not reacted in the way the "teaser" had hoped. "Teasers" want one of two reactions: to make you mad or to make you sad. If you don't react in one of these two ways, then you have taken the "air out of their balloon" (ruined their objective). If the teasing becomes excessive, this is called bullying. Be sure to tell an adult. Never keep it a secret. Bullying is dangerous.

Activity
It is so important that you stop here and take the time to allow your children to practice handling a "teaser". It's best if "Mom" or "teacher" plays the role of the "teaser" to keep the teasing safe, but allows the children to respond and practice how to handle these uncomfortable situations. Practicing these situations gives your children more confidence, which is what they need most in these situations. There are no wrong answers; just allow the children to analyze each reaction and see if it could be done differently, or if it was a great response.

Day 79
Gossiping

Gossiping includes many things, but mainly it is the "passing along" of information, which we have not been given permission to pass along. Speaking unkindly of others in any way would also fall into the category of gossiping. I want you to ask yourself this question every time you start to pass along some information: If what you're going to say to someone, could in any way cause this someone to think more negatively about the person of whom you are speaking, then that is a HUGE RED FLAG warning you not to say it. We humans tend to want others to share in our feelings, whether they are good or bad, because we like company. So when we get upset with someone,

usually it's not long before we are telling someone else about the person who made us upset. The thing is, that's not polite. You know as well as I do, that there are two sides to every story. When we go and tell someone else our side of the story, and it causes that person to think less of the person who hurt us, it's not fair. Remember, we only want to "lift" others. We don't want to be spreaders of ill thoughts or feelings, but we do want to promote good and happy feelings. This is the heart of proper etiquette. Do not participate in gossip. If someone comes to you and starts to speak ill of another, politely say, "I'm sorry. It makes me uncomfortable to listen to or talk negatively about others." Yes, it takes courage. Yes, you might be the only one who doesn't participate. However, you will reap the rewards forever. See you next time.

Activity
This is a good time to share personal experiences about when a rumor has hurt you or to allow the children (without using names) to express experiences they have had when being faced with gossip. Allow the children to "come up" with ways that they can decline to participate in gossip without hurting others' feelings. Once again, practicing this really helps.

Day 80
Potty Mouth

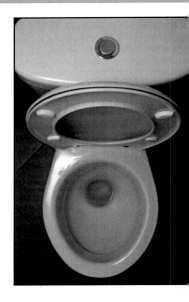

What is "Potty Mouth"? Well, use your imagination. Without getting too detailed or too disgusting, let's just agree that "potty words" and "potty talk" are things some people say that need to be discarded (thrown away). They are trash, and trash is smelly, disgusting and makes us feel dirty when we're around it, as does a "potty mouth". We have to be very careful when we speak, because our words affect the way those around us think and feel. Certain subjects are not appropriate to discuss in public. One subject that is discussed entirely too much in our society is that concerning our bodily functions. We simply do not need to talk about, or especially, ANNOUNCE when we need to perform a bodily function, or when one has just happened. Instead of announcing to our family, "If I don't get to a bathroom soon, there's going to be an unpleasant situation in the backseat of this car that I can assure you no one wants to deal with," say something like, "Mom, I think it's really important that we stop soon." Using just a little bit of tact spares everyone in the car from visualizing your current predicament, and they are grateful, trust me. Secondly, we must simply avoid all offensive language. This includes all words that are unkind, vulgar, or would be defined as a "curse word." This is a dangerous habit to get into and can affect the way others treat us. We lose the respect of our peers and adults when we show a lack of control of our tongue. Be careful, be polite. See you next time

Activity
Discussion time. Without having to list the words directly (or maybe you need to), try just discussing with your children the types of words or subjects that are not appropriate to discuss in public. Make sure you discuss why this etiquette consideration is so important (respect for others). Discuss possible consequences of participating in such discussions.

Day 81
Losing Control

I don't like to admit that I have ever "lost control," but I know that I have, and when I have, it has never turned out to be to my advantage: NEVER. Losing control of ourselves and our temper is a sign of weakness, not strength. Some people believe that the louder we speak, the more people will listen, but, actually, the opposite is true. The softer we speak, the more people will listen and respond. Think about the last time someone lost control with you. It's probably not a pleasant memory, and I only ask you to remember it to make a point, and hopefully, to help all of us want to strive to gain control over our own reactions to different and difficult circumstances. You probably felt anger, embarrassment, or sadness when someone lost control with you. It probably didn't help to encourage you to do better, but discouraged you in the end. We must strive to keep ourselves under control, to speak softly, to be gentle. Self-control under difficult or dangerous circumstances shows great strength and character, and leads to self-respect and self-worth. Sure it's easy to be kind when others are kind to us, no problem. The real test comes when others are being unkind, maybe even mean; then our true character is tested and proved. This is not easy; not for you, not for your parents, not for anyone; however we must commit to do better, to try harder and to be examples of great control in the midst of turmoil. I know you can do it. See you next time.

Activity
This can be an uncomfortable discussion for some, especially if we adults leading this discussion have a problem with staying in control of ourselves. That's OK. It's important that both our students and we remember that we are all striving to improve ourselves daily. As we learn more, we do better. These are skills that take practice and dedication. If we do a little better today, than we did yesterday, then we have made progress. Good Luck!

Day 82
Appropriate Gender Conversation

Gender means whether we are male or female. We respond differently when we are speaking to someone of our own gender than we do when speaking to someone of the opposite gender. This does not mean that etiquette considerations like "potty mouth" and "tact" are thrown out the window, just because we're talking to someone of the same gender, but there are things we need to consider, so that we can be sensitive to the expectations between the genders. For instance, if a boy were standing with a group of girls, he shouldn't bring up the subject that the pads his football team is using are causing rashes in various places on the players. The group of girls would not be interested in this subject and would probably be "grossed out." However, if you were with your fellow teammates, this would be a relevant subject to discuss. Likewise, if some girls are standing with a group of boys, the girls would not want to start discussing the problems they're having finding bathing suits that fit them correctly along with the details of the particular issues. This would simply not be appropriate conversation to have in the presence of boys; however it would be completely appropriate to have in the presence of girls only. I hope you're beginning to understand the difference. Just be sensitive to the opposite gender and think before you speak. We never want to make others feel uncomfortable or uneasy as a result of our conversation. See you next time.

Activity
This is a good time to separate the girls from the boys, and discuss on a more intimate level what we're talking about here. This is an etiquette skill that the whole world could use a refresher course in. If you ask me, we really can't talk about this enough. It's also a good time to remind the older children where the "line" is drawn, when it comes to discussing things in front of their younger siblings. Give it some thought.

Day 83
Taking Advantage

This is a subject that gets me a little "hot under the collar," if you know what I mean: taking advantage of others. As I hope we are understanding by now, true etiquette means being considerate of others; taking advantage of someone else is the worst form of improper etiquette there is. "Taking advantage" covers many things of which I will mention a few. When we take advantage of someone due to their lack of knowledge, lack of intelligence, lack of understanding, lack of means (abilities), weakened emotional state, extreme compassion or any other condition that makes them vulnerable (weak) in making a logical and sensible decision, we are in the wrong. For instance, asking our grandma, who has a difficult time telling her grandchildren "no," to buy us an expensive item, even though we know she does not have a lot of money, is taking advantage. Likewise, when someone gives us too much in "change" after a transaction, failing to give the money back or to inform the person of their error is taking advantage of someone's lack of knowledge. Once again, this type of behavior is impolite and shows poor character. Yet another example occurs when we do not disclose all relevant information that someone would need to make a proper decision. An example would be failing to give our parents all the details of a planned "outing" with friends. This is taking advantage and is a form of dishonesty. Be cautious with others, always considering the role we play as a leader in fine etiquette. See you next time.

Activity
This can be a very informative and interesting discussion. Most children think that being dishonest is telling a lie. However, as we age and mature, hopefully, we understand that dishonestly can be exhibited in many forms. Discuss with your children and use lots of examples of different forms of dishonesty: taking advantage of others, withholding information, being secretive, avoiding responsibilities, etc. Allow your children to discuss and understand why these behaviors are examples of dishonesty.

Day 84
Family Loyalty

Loyalty means to be faithful, and who better to be faithful to than our family. Family loyalty is a quality of happy and devoted families who delight in celebrating each other's accomplishments and stand firm behind each other when facing trials. Family devotion is an admirable quality and serves as a great example of impeccable etiquette. It is extremely rude to ever speak of one's own relatives in an ill or unkind manner to others, especially to those outside the family. This is an ultimate betrayal of family loyalty. Although all families have difficulties, and sometimes not everyone in the family agrees with one another, it is not polite to complain or express in public our unhappiness with certain family situations or family members. Our family needs to feel our loyalty. A great way to express family loyalty is supporting and encouraging each other in their different interests and abilities. For instance, our siblings should hear our voices over everyone else's when they are performing; whether it be on the baseball field, in a volleyball match or even in an art competition. We should be our families biggest "cheerleaders." We are also there to "soften the blow" when disappointments come. Our family members should know that when it's time to face a challenge, they will have the support of the entire family. At the same time, I do wish to state that, although it is not polite to speak unkindly of our family in public, we all need friends who, we can confide (trust) in to sometimes help us sort through family squabbles. This is not a betrayal, but we must use caution and always be respectful toward those you're speaking to and toward those you're speaking about. Finally, let me make one thing perfectly clear: when we report abuse of any kind by a family member to someone outside the family, this is not betrayal. This requires courage and could save someone's life. You are never wrong to report abuse; you are a hero. See you next time.

Activity
Please discuss loyalty and ways we can each show our families our devotion to them. Explain the difference between speaking ill of our family and expressing concern for our family. Encourage children to always remember that when abuse is divulged or reported, this is an act of heroism, not disloyalty. Reassure children that they will always be believed and supported.

Day 85
Respecting Our Siblings' Property

We all enjoy our own things and usually have certain possessions that are really special to us. Whether it's a Barbie doll or a race car, a cell phone or an I-pod, we have things that we consider ours, and we hope that others will show respect towards us, by honoring those ownerships. What does this mean, especially inside a family? Well, it means that we never take items that belong to our siblings unless we have their permission to use them. Sometimes in a family, we assume that it's OK for us to use anything and everything that is within the walls of our home. If your family has agreed to that type of sharing, then great; but often, family members still appreciate being asked before someone just takes their possessions. It's a show of courtesy and respect to politely ask before we borrow something. For girls, clothes and makeup are common items that sisters like to share. This can be so much fun, and it doubles the size of our wardrobe. Still, it is polite to ask before we take, which sends a message to our sister that we respect and appreciate her willingness to share, and we don't take it for granted (expect it). Likewise, brothers might borrow cd's, video games or other electronics. Always ask politely before taking, and then make sure we return the item when we said we would. These courtesies help keep peace in the home and allow love to be felt by all. It doesn't take long to ask, but the results go a long way in helping siblings increase their love for one another. See you next time.

Activity
Perhaps now is a good time for siblings to set up some ground rules in your home concerning borrowing and sharing. When everyone sits down and discusses these expectations and then agrees to them, there will be more peace and harmony in your home and even your classroom. As everyone thinks of their own possessions that they wish others would ask permission to use, they will have more understanding and respect for the wishes of others.

Day 86
Respecting Others' Property

We've talked earlier about respecting our siblings, property. Now let's talk about a few ways we can show respect for others' property outside of our home. When we show others that we value their possessions and property, we are demonstrating that we value them. Have you ever been tempted to take a "short cut" through someone's flower bed or ride your bike across someone's lawn? These types of behavior are considered rude because they show a lack of respect for others' property. It takes time, money and energy to plant flowers and grow a lawn; by avoiding trampling on these grounds, we show the homeowner that we value his time and money and respect his property. Graffiti is another way that we show disrespect for others' property. The only way I know that can properly compare the effects that this type of behavior has on property owners, is to have us imagine what it would feel like if someone came into our bedrooms and spray painted graffiti all over our walls and possessions. We would feel hurt and probably angry. Imagine the time and money it would take to clean and repaint our room. Anytime we abuse, destroy or are just careless with others' property, we are not showing proper etiquette and adequate respect for others. Let's consider our actions before we act. See you next time.

Activity
Have an open discussion about ways we can show respect for other people's property. This might include; not putting our feet or shoes on others' furniture, not cutting through others' yards, asking before we borrow, cleaning up after ourselves, etc. List as many ways as you can to add to discussion.

Day 87
Personal Space

What is personal space? Personal space is an invisible bubble that surrounds us, which we regard as "our space." The reason this is important to consider when thinking about proper etiquette is that we don't want to "invade" others' personal space. Usually, depending on whom we're talking to, we may increase or reduce the distance between one another. Girls usually stand closer together when speaking to one another than boys do. When talking to a stranger, we usually stand even farther away. This shows respect for others' personal space. What we want to consider with regard to etiquette is this: when we begin a conversation with someone whom we are not very familiar, it is polite to have enough space between us so that the person we're talking to does not feel uneasy. As a conversation becomes more familiar, we might find ourselves moving closer together, which is fine. When a gentleman (boy) is speaking to a lady (girl), it is always polite to stand at a comfortable distance to show respect for the lady. Of course, we would never want to stand so close to someone, that there would be a chance our saliva could end up on the one we're speaking to. This would be most unpleasant. Just try to be aware of personal space and never assume the space is smaller than you think. Think on that a moment. See you next time.

Activity
This is a fun opportunity to role play. Simply allow the children to role play proper and improper personal space. This really does help the children to become more aware of others' personal space, where as before, they probably didn't give it much thought.

Day 88
Grocery Carts and Cars

Yes, there is etiquette to be considered when dealing with grocery carts and cars. Basically, it's a great idea to always consider how our actions might affect others. For instance, have you ever finished helping your mom put groceries in the car and then returned the grocery cart to the "cart holder"? This is an act of courtesy and a show of respect for others, when we return the cart to its proper place. How? Well, a couple things could happen if we didn't return the cart. Number one, the cart could roll and hit someone else's car, which could cause a scratch or dent. Number two, when the cart is left between or in a parking place, it could prevent others from being able to park in those places. Third, when the carts are left all over the parking lot, it makes the job of the grocery store employees that much harder, because they have to run all over the parking lot collecting carts. This is probably extremely frustrating on cold or rainy days. So you see, one act of consideration from us, can help show respect to other's property as well as their time. Another way that we can remember to show our respect for others' property is when we open our car doors. We need to always be gentle when opening car doors, whether getting in or getting out. This helps ensure that we don't accidentally hit someone else's car with our door, which can cause dents and scratches. Let's be careful and considerate when using grocery carts and opening car doors; both are great ways to show great manners. See you next time.

Day 89
Disposing of Trash Properly

Another act of courtesy is when we dispose of our trash properly. It makes me sad when I drive down the streets of my city and see all the trash littering the sides of the road. This is unattractive and shows a complete disregard for the beauty of the earth. It seems so simple to discard our trash properly; there are trash cans everywhere. Cities and states spend thousands of dollars that could be spent on many more uplifting programs than cleaning up others' trash. By disposing of our trash properly, we show our respect for not only this earth, but for others. No one likes to look out their window and see garbage. We would be horrified if we woke up one morning and walked out our front door to find our yard littered with garbage. Sometimes people don't consider the effects of being careless with just one piece of trash. However, if thousands of people are careless with one piece of trash, then we have tons of garbage littering our cities. Let's put forth a considerable effort to make sure we are not responsible for any litter. We can all feel better when we know that we are responsible for helping our towns and cities remain beautiful places to admire and enjoy. See you next time.

Activity
This is a great time to discuss recycling and the effects this has on our society. Educate yourselves on ways that you and your family can participate in recycling. Exchange ideas on how to make recycling convenient and simple, so that the whole family can participate. A great experiment is to discard all recyclable material for one week into a separate garbage can (cans). At the end of the week, weigh your recyclable trash. Multiply that by 52. Now your family can see the real effect of recycling. What a difference just one family can make!

Day 90
Visiting Others' Homes

There are many things to consider when visiting others' homes. Of course, we always want to be on our best behavior when we are a guest in someone's home. There are some etiquette considerations that I'm sure you are probably already familiar with; however, I'm going to list them so that they can be reviewed and reconsidered. Just keep in mind, when we are a guest in someone's home we observe these considerations:

1. **We only eat in the designated areas.**
2. **We never enter rooms with closed doors.**
3. **We always knock before entering a bathroom.**
4. **We always check our shoes for cleanliness, sometimes removing them if necessary.**
5. **We never open refrigerators, cabinets, or closets without permission.**
6. **We never put our feet on furniture.**
7. **We never climb on, roll over, stand or bounce on furniture.**
8. **We never answer the phone without permission.**
9. **We always clean up after ourselves.**
10. **We always make our beds and keep our guest room tidy.**
11. **We always hang up bath towels.**
12. **We never open windows or change thermostats without permission.**
13. **We never have our music or TV so loud, that it would disturb others.**
14. **We always offer to help prepare meals, etc.**

When visiting others, these considerations are great ways to make sure we're invited back. Use your best judgment when other situations arise, and enjoy being a guest. See you next time.

Activity
Go through this list one by one and allow the children to ask and understand why these behaviors might be considered rude. If it's our grandparents' home or another home where we are a frequent guest, some of these behaviors might be acceptable. However, it is a good idea to discuss them and make sure they are all considered carefully.

Day 91
Riding in Others' Cars

This etiquette consideration is similar to those we observe when visiting other's homes. However, let's think about the details of this etiquette consideration. Whenever we are riding in someone else's car, we want to be very careful that we show respect and appreciation for the car and for the owners of that car. Unless we have been given permission, we never want to eat or drink in others' cars. If we are given permission, let's be extra careful that we don't have spills or drop food. Before entering someone's car, we should always check our shoes to make sure there is not an extreme amount of dirt, mud or other foreign objects on our shoes. When exiting the car, we need to double check to see if there is any trash or other personal items being left behind. We want to leave the car in the same way that we found it. We can show respect to the driver of the car by not being too loud or too active, as this can be distracting to the driver and possibly even dangerous. Let's be kind, by not complaining about the music or other forms of "car entertainment" that the driver provides. Getting in someone else's car and immediately asking them to turn on the radio or to switch the station to a different one is rude. It is polite to simply accept the choice of the driver. We want to be a welcome guest while riding in others' cars. See you next time.

Activity
Now is a great time for the kids to put together a "car box". It doesn't necessarily have to be a box, but any container where the children can place great games or activities that can be used in a car. For instance, coloring books or drawing paper, pencils and crayons, crossword or sudoku puzzles, word searches, books, small toys, etc. would serve the purpose. There's a lot less arguing and disagreements when everyone has something to do. Have fun creating your car box.

Day 92
Pet Etiquette

I am a pet lover. I have two dogs whom I adore. I know lots of you are pet lovers also. However, not everyone loves pets, and, even when they do, we must still consider ways to make sure our pets are not a nuisance to others. If we keep our pets outside, we should consider keeping them behind fences, so that they are not tempted to "invade" the property of others. I have a friend who lives out in the country next to a neighbor who has two large dogs. These dogs regularly come into my friend's yard and have caused her to be afraid to go out into her own yard. This neighbor's behavior in not controlling his dogs is both irresponsible and inconsiderate. Even if we do keep our dogs outside in a fenced-in area, we need to make sure their barking is not excessive (too much). This can be very annoying to neighbors, disrupting conversations, naps, relaxation and other enjoyments we are all entitled (deserve) to in our own homes. If we take our dogs for a walk, we must make sure we have them on a leash, unless it is in a "dog free/no leash" park. We have to consider that many

people are afraid of dogs and do not feel safe around unleashed dogs. We need to respect and honor leash laws to show our condideration of others. Finally, we want to clean up after our dogs. If we take our dogs into public places, we must carry with us adequate supplies so that we can clean up after dog accidents. Nothing is more disgusting then stepping into "doggy doo doo." Be considerate of others in regard to all your pets, never imposing (forcing) your pets on others. See you next time.

Activity
Now is a great time to discuss pet etiquette. Make sure the children understand their responsibility as a pet owner. Think of ways to help ensure that your pet is not a nuisance to others. Making a "pet chart" is a great way to divide up the responsibilities of a family's pet (pets). Include on your chart responsibilities such as feeding, watering, grooming, bathing, exercising, walking, teaching, etc. Rotate these responsibilities so that everyone can learn how to properly care for their pets.

Day 93
Swimming Pool Etiquette

Where I live, summer is around the corner. I love the smell of suntan lotion, because it reminds me of sunshine, "pool side," and having fun. Although I do believe that if you're going to hang around the pool, you shouldn't get upset if you get a little wet, we still need to be considerate of others who are in or near the pool. Remembering pool etiquette is not only polite; it also keeps everyone at the pool more safe, which is very important. We should realize that the bigger we get, the more we need to be aware of those who are smaller than we are. Bigger kids should never play right next to smaller children at the pool. This is a good way for little kids to get hurt or become frightened. Remember, we are always trying to help others feel more comfortable, and helping them feel safer is another polite etiquette consideration. We tend to get really excited when we are swimming, because it's so much fun; however, this can lead to accidents involving others, especially little children. If we are going to be jumping in the water practicing our latest "cannonballs", we should pick a place at the pool that is less crowded and away from people lying by the pool. This prevents injuries, as well as annoyed sunbathers. If you take a radio

to the pool, always ask those around you if they mind if you play it. This shows consideration of others and doesn't assume that everyone will like your music. Also, remember that taking toys to the pool is great fun, but usually toys at the pool get "passed around" from one kid to the next. So make sure that if you take a toy or float to the pool, it's something that you don't mind sharing. Have fun in the sun, and always be safe. See you next time.

Activity
Since we're talking about swimming, now is a great time to talk about swimming pool safety, including CPR. Take this time to review CPR, and allow all your children to practice by verbally speaking the steps and showing you the procedure. There are great CPR videos via the web that you can watch with your children. Talk about other pool safety, such as diving in shallow water, running, horseplay and other dangers around water.

Day 94
Music, TV and Movie Etiquette

We all have our favorite music, TV shows and movies. I'm kind of a country music fan and a fan of "sappy love stories." I don't watch a lot of TV, so I can't comment on TV shows, but I do enjoy watching a little news each day. What if I come to your house tomorrow and we spend the whole day watching love stories and listening to country music. Wow, that sounds awesome doesn't it? No….What…..You don't like watching sappy love stories? Come on, who doesn't love a great love story? OK. I hope you're getting the idea of how it would feel to be forced to listen to or watch something that you don't enjoy and maybe don't even feel comfortable watching. We must consider those we are with before we turn to a certain radio station or put on a certain movie. Asking those we're with how they feel about the entertainment we want to watch or listen to with them, is a great way to show respect for their opinions and their values. Some people don't believe in watching anything violent whatsoever, so putting on a war movie would be inconsiderate of their feelings and values. There are particular boys who might go into "spasms" if they are forced to watch a show about decorating cupcakes, so we would want to consider this before we sit next to them. The point is, don't force your own likes and dislikes of entertainment on others. There is so much variety when it comes to entertainment, that I know you and your family or your friends can reach a compromise when it comes to choosing entertainment. Finally when choosing entertainment, don't ever lower your standards when you're with others. Be strong, be courageous, and be able to feel good about your choices. See you next time.

Activity
This is a great time to discuss the family's or student's standards in entertainment, and ways to help students have the courage to uphold their own standards when being faced with entertainment choices. It's so hard to be the only one who doesn't want to watch a certain movie or listen to a certain radio station; however being different is being brave. Allow the students to discuss experiences they have had in this regard, and allow other students to give feedback on better ways to handle different situations. This is also a good topic to role play. Allow the kids to practice what they can say when they don't agree with the choice in entertainment.

Day 95
Proper Etiquette During Entertainment

Many of our etiquette considerations overlap each other, so at times you will feel like we've already covered certain subjects. However, I think it's important to be as specific as possible when it comes to etiquette. I do not believe for one minute that you are not capable of thinking for yourself and determining what is proper and what is not. Like I said earlier, if we always keep other people's feelings in mind, we will never have to worry about our etiquette skills. I have found, however, that sometimes someone will mention a certain behavior that I have not considered to be actually rude, but when it is mentioned in a particular way, I think to myself, "Wow, that might cause someone to feel uneasy, and I've never thought about it in that particular way before." I hope that is what happens as you read this manual. Now on to entertainment. As you know, when we are watching a performance of any kind, whether it is a movie, a play, a symphony, etc, we need to be courteous to those around us. This includes not using our cell phones and making sure the ring tone is turned off, not making any annoying noises like tapping our feet or rattling papers, and not talking and whispering during the performance. Eating too loudly, especially with crunchy foods like popcorn and potato chips, can be extremely distracting to those around us. As we are courteous to others, we hope that these favors will be returned to us, so that we can all enjoy the entertainment. See you next time.

Activity
Grab a book off the shelf and assign one student to read one paragraph from the book. Before he/she begins reading, however, tell the students around them to begin whispering into each other's ears, telling stories and anything else they can think to say. Now the reading begins. After the reader has finished the paragraph, allow the reader to express his/her feelings about this experiment. Allow all the students to try. Hopefully, they will realize that even quiet whispering can disturb someone's concentration. This can be extremely frustrating, especially when someone has paid money to see a performance. Something to think about.

Day 96
Entering & Exiting Rows

Entering and exiting a row of spectators at a performance can be tricky and a little unnerving (uncomfortable); however, with a few reminders, we can do this politely and courteously, avoiding any uncomfortable situations. The first consideration to remember when passing in front of people, is to face the stage or screen, pressing close to the backs of the seats. While you pass others, it is polite to say "excuse me." It is not necessary for people to stand to let you pass, but if they do, say, "Thank you." It's usually appropriate for gentlemen to stand so ladies can pass in front of them. Try your best not to step on any toes or personal items. Also, be careful not to drag things across people's heads, like coats, purses and bags. If you can, wait until intermissions or pauses in the performance to exit and enter a row. Also, limit the number of times you get up and down during a performance. If you know you are someone who has to get up and down more often, try to get a seat on the end of the row. Finally, never wear hats or other items of clothing that would prevent others from being able to see the performance. As always, use your best judgment, and enjoy your entertainment. See you next time.

Day 97
Etiquette While Playing Games

As you know, games are supposed to be fun and enjoyable, but misbehavior during play can result in hurt feelings. It's hard not to let our competitive nature (our desire to win) come out when playing games. Yet, if we remember our etiquette, it will help us to be able to enjoy the entire experience more fully and provide others more enjoyment as well. Here is a list of etiquette considerations to remember the next time we play a game with others, in order to ensure everyone's enjoyment:

1. **Never criticize, or even seem aware of other's mistakes.**

2. **If you lose, don't make "sneering" remarks, blaming the other person's win on luck, etc.**

3. **If you win, don't brag about your extreme intelligence or abilities, etc.**

4. **Never act disappointed to have a particular person on your team.**

5. **Always congratulate winners.**

6. **Don't make excuses for your loss, like blaming others.**

7. **Know the rules of the game and the proper etiquette of a sport.**

8. **Don't engage in sulking, pouting, explaining, complaining, protesting, etc.**

9. **Play for the sake of playing, not winning.**

The 10th rule and most important etiquette consideration you could ever live by when playing games is this: Be a cheerful loser and a quiet winner.

See you next time.

Activity
You know what they say: practice makes perfect. Pull out a board game and let's put these etiquette considerations to the test. Make sure the students are familiar with all the game etiquette considerations and then instruct them that their final test for the day is how well they practice it. Even knowing these considerations, it's really hard to abide by them. Be an encourager to the students, congratulating them and complimenting their polite behavior.

Day 98
Being a Spectator at a Sporting Event

I love to go and watch my favorite football team play, but what I love even more is going to watch my children and my friends' children play sports. It's so much fun to "cheer on" those we love and celebrate their accomplishments and their excitement in their team. I must admit, however, that sometimes I am disappointed in the way a few fans misbehave, which can make it unpleasant for those trying to watch the event. That's why I want to discuss a few etiquette considerations regarding being a spectator. Here are few guidelines to consider:

1. **Arrive at the game on time, so that we don't distract fans when getting into our seats.**

2. **Try to stay seated during play (wait for breaks in play to get up and down).**

3. **Don't stop the flow of traffic—if you see someone you know who you haven't seen in a long time—move to the side, so that people can continue walking**

4. **Make sure you don't "cut" in front of others. Ask if you're not sure.**

5. **Wear school or team colors to show support for your team.**

6. **LET THE COACHES COACH—yelling directions to a child from the stands causes confusion and sends too many messages to the child. It also sends a message to the coach that you don't trust his/her coaching ability.**

7. **Never complain in front of others about how a particular child is playing.**

8. **Yell only positive remarks from stands—keep negative ones to yourself.**

9. **Never make fun of, sneer at, or laugh at those playing.**

10. **Congratulate everyone on a great game!**

Be a great fan!!!! See you next time.

Activity
Today is a great day to make family "cheer" signs. Make a special sign for each child that can be taken to their sporting events, academic events or any type of performance event. Each child should make a sign for a sibling. They shouldn't make their own sign. Use poster board, wood handles, paint, glitter, etc. to make a sign every child can be proud of. Have fun and Cheer, Cheer, Cheer!

Day 99
Playground Etiquette

Playgrounds, no doubt, are for running, jumping, sliding and basically acting like a little monkey. It's nice to be able to go someplace, where we can play without having to worry about how loud we are. Kids don't like being quiet, do they? Although, like most parents, we just want you to have fun and enjoy being a kid when you're on the playground, safety is still a consideration. Here are a few suggestions to consider:

- **Big kids look out for little kids. Sometimes we big kids forget how huge we can appear to a little toddler. Be careful that we don't run over or into little kids while we're running around having fun.**

- **It's best not to throw rocks. This is the source of more tears than I care to count. Even though we don't mean to, it seems a rock always ends up somewhere it's not supposed to, like in someone's eye or face. This can really hurt and cause serious injury. Don't throw rocks.**

- **Take turns…need I say more?**

- **Don't walk up slides unless no one is waiting to slide down.**

- **Keep pets away from playgrounds—remember those who are afraid of pets, especially little children.**

- **Do not eat or drink on playground equipment.**

- **Check weight and size limit before using playground equipment.**

Have fun and be safe. See you next time.

Activity
Come On! Get up and go to a Playground. Why not? It's fun! It's the only way to practice playground etiquette.

Day 100
Acts of Kindness Towards Ladies (this includes girls)

Yes, I mean all females. Etiquette towards ladies is a polite tradition and one I would love to see more of. Sometimes, gentlemen (boys) might feel like this is unfair. Where are the etiquette considerations shown to gentlemen by ladies? Well, all I can tell you gentlemen is that showing extra kindness to ladies will "pay off" (give great benefits) for you a "hundred fold" (you will get back more than you give). Trust me on this. It is polite for gentlemen to hold the door open for ladies. If you are behind a lady, it is extremely courteous if you quickly get in front of her, so that you may open the door for her. If you are someplace where the seats are all taken, for instance riding on a bus, and a lady arrives, it is polite for a gentleman to give her his seat. It is considerate for a gentleman to allow a lady to hold his arm or hold his hand while walking, especially if the lady is wearing high heels, so she isn't likely to fall. Helping a lady to put on her coat is also very polite. Gentlemen show great etiquette when they help a lady to her seat or when they stand when she exits the table. These are a few etiquette considerations that gentlemen can show to ladies. When these considerations are shown, I hope that all ladies will express sincere gratitude for these acts of kindness. See you next time.

Activity
Discuss this in more detail. For some young men, the thought of performing these acts of kindness towards ladies is embarrassing; however as they grow and mature, it will become easier and more comfortable. However, if these considerations are taught at very young ages, then it will become "second nature." As always, learning by example is the best way to learn. Hopefully dads, grandpas and other male adults in your child's life are great examples of etiquette towards ladies.

Day 101
Acts Of Kindness Towards The Elderly

Our elderly are one of our greatest assets (benefits). Honoring them through daily acts of kindness is a wonderful way to help show them how much we appreciate their life and their example to us. Those who have "walked the path" before us, have much wisdom that can be passed along to us if we will but listen. Imagine that you are walking down a long and winding trail through the forest. Ahead of you, but out of your sight, is a pit covered by leaves that a troll has set for you. As you walk along, beside the trail sits a feeble old man who doesn't appear to even see you. Just before you fall into the pit, the old man yells, "Watch your step boy, there's a hidden trap just in front of you. You might want to take the other path." Now, you knew that there was another path, but you didn't want to take it, because it was longer and had more hills to climb. What do you think you would do? Do you believe the old man? Does he even know what he's talking about? "He's probably just day dreaming," you might think. The elderly have already learned many things as they have gone through life. Listen to them, learn from them, honor them. A few ways we can show honor to the elderly are these: help them carry things, hold their hand or arm with they walk, assist them in and out of cars and through doors, visit and call them regularly, ask them questions about their lives, love them, and let them know how important they are to you. See you next time.

Activity

Let's go visit a nursing home. What a great way to honor the elderly. Take the whole family or whole class to the nearest nursing home, be on your best behavior, and go visit the elderly. When we go, we simply walk into someone's room and ask, "Would you care for any company?" Rarely do we get a "no". We go in and introduce ourselves, and then we ask about them and their lives. We share with them about our family and simply have a nice conversation. We try not to stay more than 10-15 minutes, so that we don't tire them out too much. We thank them for allowing us to visit and express our gratitude for their kindness. It's so much fun. Try it….you'll want to do it again.

Day 102
Etiquette Towards Those With Disabilities

The information that I wish to give you on this topic comes directly from people who suffer with disabilities. These individuals wish to educate others on the polite way to treat, speak to, and associate with those with disabilities. Sometimes, things can be said unintentionally that are hurtful to someone suffering with a disability. First of all, people with disabilities are not the condition or the disability; rather they are individual human beings who are suffering with the disability. For example, we would never say, "Did you know John is an epileptic?" Instead, we would say, "John has epilepsy." When talking to someone with a disability, regardless of what the disability is, look and speak directly to the person, not through someone else. For instance, if you're standing by someone in a wheelchair and you want to ask if she's had a good day, don't ask her mom who is standing beside her if she's had a good day, but ask the girl directly. It's also polite to get at eye level with the person you are talking to. This prevents them from having to lift up their head every time they speak to someone. If you're speaking to someone with a severe loss of vision, identify yourself and those around you, for instance, "Hi, John, it's me, David. Emily is on my right and Jason is on my left." Always ask before you help someone with a disability, for instance, "Jennifer would you like me to help you open that bottle? They can be awfully hard to open." Be sensitive to those suffering with disabilities, but treat them as real individuals who are just like you and me, because they are. See you next time.

Activity
A great experience that your whole family can learn from is meeting and getting to know someone with a disability. If you know someone who suffers from a disability, call them and ask them if they would be interested in helping your children (class) understand better the challenges that affect people with disabilities, along with the great accomplishments that can be achieved as well. As we all understand each other better, our challenges and our dreams, our compassion for one another grows, and we start to see how much we all have in common. Before the meeting, it's a good idea to write down some questions that the students are interested in, in case students become "shy" during the meeting.

Day 103
Etiquette When Friends Come Over

I know that we all love it when friends come over. It means PAR.....TYYYYY! We've already talked about proper etiquette when we are the visitor at another person's home, but what about when we are the host? What are some polite considerations we can offer our guests to make sure that their visit to our home is fun and enjoyable? Here are a few: First, it's important to introduce our guests to everyone in our home. This prevents our guests from later meeting a "stranger" in the hallway and feeling uncomfortable. Second, we always want to make sure our guests are never hungry. Just because we're not hungry, doesn't mean our guests aren't. Inform our guests of what time meals will be served and then ask if they need a snack to "hold them over" until meal time. Another polite consideration is to ask our guests if the temperature in our home is comfortable for them. If they are too cool or too warm, we can always offer a sweater or perhaps adjust the thermostat. It's always polite to let our guests select forms of entertainment, like what movie to watch or which video game to play. This demonstrates to our guests our appreciation for them and for their visit. Making our guests feel special can be a lot of fun and can ensure that they will want to visit us again in the near future. Enjoy your guests. I know I will enjoy mine. See you next time.

Activity
Brainstorm about different ways your family can make your next guest feel special and comfortable in your home. I've seen families make meal cards that have a few choices for each meal, and just like in the hotels, their guests are given the cards at night for the next day's meals, and the guest marks his/her choices. The card is then given to the host to prepare the meals. Wow, that would really make your guest feel like they were on a real vacation. Think of other things that you really appreciate when you're on vacation, and try to incorporate a few of these ideas into your next guest's visit. This can be a lot fun

Day 104
Guest Room or Guest Basket

I get so excited when I'm preparing for guests to arrive to my home. If you have a guest room, you can add a few items to the room to help your guest feel comfortable and well cared for. If you don't have a designated guest room, don't worry. You can make any room in the house a guest room by adding a "guest basket" and a few other items. Here are a few suggestions to add to your room or basket:

- Coat hangers
- Extra blankets
- Candles and matches
- Body lotions and bath soaps with wonderful smells
- Suntan lotion
- Bed light
- Bath soaps
- Good books or magazines
- Mirror and table (for grooming)
- Alarm clock
- Morning paper
- Pen and paper
- Snacks

Making a guest basket can be so much fun. These items help our guest feel special and will make them pleased that they stayed in our "hotel" rather than another. Have fun preparing for your guests. See you next time.

Activity
Find a basket or some type of container. Place some colorful tissue paper, fabrics or anything to add some color and pizzazz to it, and start filling it with some of the suggestions above and anything else your family decides would be great to add. This will really get your family "pumped up" and excited to host a guest. After you're done, place some saran wrap or some type of cover on it so that nothing gets, dusty and await the arrival of your next guest. Enjoy.

Day 105
Being a Good Neighbor

When you live near other people, either right next door, somewhere in your apartment building, or even on the same street, they are your neighbors. There are several etiquette considerations that we need to keep in mind, so that we can be great neighbors. How can we be great neighbors and demonstrate neighborly etiquette? For starters, we can keep our yards clean and neat. This means not leaving our toys, bikes, balls and other play equipment scattered around the yard or driveway. Also, we can keep our lawn properly mowed, trimmed and free from too many weeds and unsightly growths so that our yard will not be an "eye sore" for our neighbors (an ugly thing to look at). Keeping our homes clean and tidy on the outside, expresses our respect for our neighbors and their property. If we live in an apartment building, we can strive to keep the area around our front door, as well as our porches, clean and free from trash. When new neighbors move into our neighborhood, it's very polite to go quickly and introduce our family. Welcome the newcomers into the neighborhood with homemade bread, cookies, or other treats. Try to stay informed about your neighbors, so that you will know when they need extra help in case of health issues, financial issues, or other circumstances that might require some extra TLC (tender loving care). Being a great neighbor definitely has its rewards: great friends, good times and lots of love. See you next time.

Activity

This is a great opportunity to do something for a neighbor. Look around your street or building and identify a neighbor whom your family does not know very well. Make a treat of some kind, and with the whole family, walk over and say "hello." Introduce your family, deliver the "goodies", and invite your new friends to come over for a "game night," or perhaps some ice cream. Another great idea is to organize a street party for your street or building. Make invitations for a "Get To Know You" party and invite everyone to bring "potluck" and come and enjoy some fellowship. This is a great way to transform your street or building into a real "home."
Have fun and BE BRAVE!

Day 106
Etiquette in the Classroom

OK, kids, we are more than 2/3 through with this etiquette manual. Wow, we're making great progress! I'm really proud of the way you are "hanging in there" and being consistent with your etiquette study. I hope your entire family is talking more about etiquette on a daily basis and I also hope you are recognizing situations where you can practice your etiquette considerations. That's when you know you are really learning. One place that I would really like to see improvement in our etiquette skills is in the classroom. Classroom settings can be full of learning and very uplifting, or they can be difficult and discouraging for both the teacher and the student. What makes a class enjoyable is when everyone feels like they are learning things that will help them in their life and when there are no distractions that inhibit (stop) this learning from taking place. One thing I know for sure is that NO LEARNING IS EVER WASTED! That's impossible. You might not believe that yet, but I can assure you that the only way to waste knowledge; is to do nothing with it. It's your choice. How can we make sure we are getting the most out of a class? Participate and listen. How do we listen? Our eyes should be on the instructor when he/she is teaching. Looking around, playing with "whatever", daydreaming, etc. are all rude behaviors that tell the instructor you are not interested in what he/she is saying. Creating any type of distraction is also rude, because this behavior tells your classmates that you don't care whether they can hear the instructor or not. Be a great student, and show respect and kindness to your instructor and your fellow students by paying attention, not talking during instruction, keeping your eyes on the instructor, answering questions and quietly following directions. All these actions ensure that you will get the most out of your class. See you next time.

Activity
The best way to teach children the importance of classroom etiquette is to allow them to be the teacher for a day (or an hour, etc.). Give your student(s) a lesson to study, prepare and share with the class. It would be helpful if the lesson material deals with a subject that is of interest to the "temporary teacher." This will help them to get excited about sharing the material with the rest of the class. Then allow them to teach. Don't give the rest of the class any specific instructions for behavior; just allow things to "unfold" as they may. This is a great way for children to experience the "ups and downs" of teaching and will hopefully "open their eyes" to the need for them to have excellent behavior when they are the student. Give it a try.

Day 107
Respect for Mom and Dad

Showing respect and honor to our mom and dad is a great way to show that we really understand and have embraced the "art of etiquette." Our parents love us; if they didn't, they wouldn't be trying to teach us skills to improve our lives. How we treat our moms and dads is a great indicator (sign) of how we will treat our families in the future. Learning to treat our families with love and respect doesn't just happen automatically. It actually takes time, determination, and a decision by us to do our part to help ensure that our relationships with our parents are loving, safe and enduring. There are obviously many ways we can show respect for our parents, but I will mention only a few. Listening to and obeying our parents are great ways we can show respect and love for them. By so doing, we let our parents know that we trust and believe in them. Our parents our responsible for our safety and wellbeing. They make decisions based on that

responsibility every day, and it is a child's responsibility to honor those decisions and show gratitude for them, even when we don't agree. Serving our parents is another great way to show respect for them. Do you ever consider the acts of service your parents provide for you? You might just think that what they do for you is their responsibility, "That's what parents' do.", and you are correct. However, the manner in which parents fulfill these responsibilities is up to them, and it is all an act of service. Yes, most parents love serving their children. This doesn't mean, however, our parents wouldn't appreciate hearing "thank you," or wouldn't love their children to find ways to help serve in the home without being asked. Love and honor your parents, and watch the great blessings that blossom from these relationships. See you next time.

Activity
It's time for a competition. For one week (or even one day if it's all you can survive), time your children. Each time you ask one of them to complete any task, start timing them from the second you asked to the second they began the task. Try to do this without their knowledge. Record these times for one week. At the end of one week, have a family council. Discuss the importance of "obeying first request" and why having to be asked more than once to complete a task is a sign of disrespect. Express these thoughts with love and tenderness, encouraging and asking your children to try to do better. Finally, it's time for the rewards: the child with the lowest combined times for the week gets the "biggest" prize, and then the other gifts are given according to their place in the outcome. You might get cries of, "It's not fair; we didn't know" (which I think is very comical). However, "stick to your guns," and let them know that without their knowledge, there will be more days when time is important.

Day 108
Keeping Our Rooms Clean

Keeping our rooms clean and neat is a polite way to show respect for our home, our parents, and the things which we own. Why? Well, our parents work very hard to provide us with the things we enjoy. Our parents also do their best to keep the things we have in good condition and working properly. When or if we keep our own rooms neat and tidy, it shows that we appreciate our things, and we don't take our things for granted (show of ingratitude). When our moms and dads don't have to worry about our room's cleanliness, they are more free to concentrate on the rest of the house, which helps them with their time. I know that your parents appreciate all you do to keep your room clean. Organizing our rooms so we have a specific place for everything, helps us keep it clean. Once a year, going through our rooms to see if there is anything we have outgrown or things we don't need anymore, is a great way to help those less fortunate than we are. Donating these unused and unneeded items to charity is a great way to help our community. Be proud of your room, and make it a haven for you and those you share it with. See you next time.

Activity
OK, yes, you know what today's activity is going to be: clean your rooms. Don't just clean your room, however; let's organize it. We might need to "rethink" the way we have things organized. It might be time to go through toys, clothes, and other items that we could possibly give away, thus freeing up some space. Plastic drawers, file folders, storage boxes, and shelving are great places to store and organize multiple items. Allow the children to come up with their own ideas for storing, and be creative. There are some great, fun ideas that make storage look like designer décor. Have fun and Enjoy!!!

Day 109
Polite Etiquette in "Houses of Worship"

Do you know what "sacred" means? It refers to something which is held in the highest esteem and is valued above all else. To hold something sacred is to protect it from intrusions or disrespect from those who do not consider sacred. Many people hold sacred their houses of worship, whether it is a church, a mosque, a synagogue, etc. Out of respect for those who regard these places sacred, we should always be reverent when entering these houses of worship, as well as while we are there. As we show respect for these buildings, we are showing respect to those who hold them sacred. When we enter and visit these buildings, we should be quiet, walk softly, speak in "hushed" tones, fold our arms and do our best not to distract from the services taking place. It's not important whether we believe the activities or services are of a sacred nature. What is important, is that we recognize that the people who are participating in the service do. Proper etiquette always requires us to help make others feel valued and at ease. By honoring their traditions and their beliefs, we honor them. See you next time.

Activity
Many houses of worship are beautifully decorated and works of art in and of themselves. Find out if there is a time when a local church, mosque or synagogue is available for visitors. Most leaders of these buildings would be happy to tell visitors about their buildings, explaining their uses, the purpose of symbols and providing general knowledge concerning their houses of worship. This is a great opportunity to increase our students' understanding, compassion, and love for other people and tolerance of other faiths.

Day 110
Removal of Hats

The etiquette rules involving hats used to be quite varied, because of the popularity of hats. Today, hats are not worn as often and are not used to measure one's status in society (economic level) like they were at one time. Years ago, people would look and see how nice, tall or different someone's hat was, in order to determine if they were from the "lower classes" or the "upper classes." So, having a nice hat was very important. So where did the removal of the hat as a sign of respect or politeness come from? Well, at the turn of the twentieth century, when so many were wearing hats, it became a polite gesture to "tip your hat" when greeting someone, especially a lady. It was considered part of the greeting, a show of respect. Thus, came the phrase, "I tip my hat to you," which means, "Well done; I respect what you've done." This polite tradition became the tradition of never wearing your hat in the presence of a lady and removing it at the dinner table and in other

intimate settings. Today, we still "hang on" to a few of those traditions regarding the hat. Now, about the only hats I see are baseball hats. Nevertheless, let's discuss a few "hat rules" so we never get in trouble wearing our hats. Number one, always remove your hat before you sit down to dine at a table. Number two, always remove your hat when being introduced to others, especially ladies. Number three, never wear a hat into a wedding, funeral or religious service unless the hat is part of the religious service. Number four, never allow your hat to be a nuisance to others (blocking vision, being disruptive). These etiquette rules will keep you "out of the dog house" when it comes to wearing your hat, and are courtesies that everyone will appreciate. See you next time.

Activity
Have some fun and look up the history of hats. There's a lot. Give each student the assignment of finding unique information about hats, like different hats for different purposes, different hats for different "classes of people," different hats for different religious services, etc. Allow everyone to draw, color, or paint a picture of the most interesting hat they found and describe its purpose. A little history lesson.

Day 111
While Walking…

Yes, there really is etiquette to be considered while walking. No, I'm not getting "carried away." You would be surprised at the irritation and frustration some people can experience while walking down the street because of the lack of consideration of others, especially on busy streets. Let's consider a few of these, so that we are not guilty of irritating others. A really sweet consideration that gentlemen can offer ladies while walking down the street, is for the gentlemen to always take the "curb side" of the sidewalk. This is simply a consideration for her safety and the safety of her clothes. Whether it's a car that drives too close to the sidewalk, or a car that hits a large puddle of water, this polite gesture can go a long way in securing the appreciation of a lady (hint, hint). Next, while walking along in public, we should keep our voice volume at a low level so that we don't impose (force) our conversation on others. Speaking about personal matters, including finances, or health concerns, is not an appropriate conversation to have on the sidewalk where others can hear. Attracting attention to ourselves while walking, by using a loud voice, wearing loud or obnoxious clothes, staring at people, knocking into them, or, talking "across" others would all be considered rude behavior. Last, sidewalks are usually intended only for walking. Most sidewalks have signs that prohibit bikes, skateboards and other transportation equipment. Be considerate of these rules, because they are designed to keep everyone safe. See you next time.

Day 112
A Sign of Respect for a Lady

A very important and polite etiquette consideration that all gentlemen, regardless of age, should follow is this; a gentleman should never enter the home of a lady when no one else is home. This is a rule of respect, a rule of value and a rule of safety. Out of respect for the lady and for her reputation, a gentleman would never do anything that might compromise a lady's good name in the judgment of others. What does this mean for us? It means that a boy does not go into a girl's home unless her parents are at home. This not only demonstrates our regard for our friend, but it also expresses our regard for our friend's parents and their home. It is rude for anyone to enter someone's home without the owner's inviting them. Keeping this in mind is a great way to ensure that we are always welcome, because we always honor the authority of our friend's parents. For your safety and the safety of your female friend, be faithful in keeping this etiquette consideration. Sometimes it will take great strength and fortitude (courage) to do this; however, I know that you will gain the respect of not only the parents of your friend, but that of your friend, as well. See you next time.

Activity
This is a good time to discuss our responsibility and the need for us to understand how our actions affect not only ourselves, but others. It is important that both boys and girls take responsibility for not placing their friends in awkward or inappropriate situations. This conversation should be an ongoing one that we have with our children. As they grow and mature, we can become more specific with the "whys" and "why-nots" of these considerations. Something I often tell my son is, "It is your responsibility that you never contribute to someone else making a poor decision". Allow this conversation to expand as your children ask more questions.

Day 113
Never Take More Than Your Share

We already touched on this subject when we were talking about buffet lines. However, this consideration travels much further than buffet lines; it reaches into many different situations. For instance, imagine you enter a bus and want to sit down, but there are not any seats available. You look around, and then you realize that some seats have only one person sitting in them, but all their stuff takes up the other seat. This would be referred to as "hogging," taking more than our share. Imagine again that you go to the library to start on your book report. You find a book and then look for a table, so that you can work on your report. You locate a table with four chairs. However, the one person sitting at the table has papers and books spread out over the entire table, preventing anyone else from using it. Once again, this would be considered "hogging." Let's not be a "hogger." Let's make sure that we don't take more than our share of anything, such as food, space, time, or money. Think about it. See you next time.

Activity
Take the time to allow the children to think of ways we can be a "hog." As they learn to recognize this behavior, hopefully, they will learn to appreciate a more frugal lifestyle. Imagine what this world would be like if no one took more than "their share." Discuss it.

Day 114
Removal of Coats

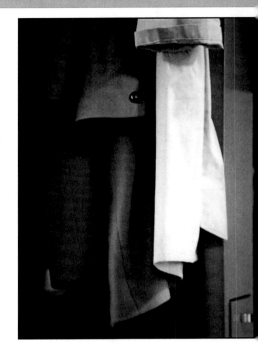

It is always polite to help the elderly and women with removing and putting on their coats. Coats can be heavy and burdensome, so a little extra help with them is always appreciated. Can you imagine how pleased your mom would feel, when upon entering a restaurant, as she began to remove her coat, you said, "Allow me to help you with that Mom," and then you went and hung it up? Your mother would be glowing with pride as this small act of service "spoke" of your love and admiration for her. It doesn't take much to express your devotion to others. Small, simple acts of kindness go a long way in developing and maintaining strong relationships that bring joy to the giver as well as the receiver. In addition to helping with coats, offering to walk along holding an umbrella over the head of a lady or an elderly person, is another courtesy that is much appreciated. Words can never equal acts of kindness. See you next time.

Activity

Allow everyone to share a time when someone performed a small act of kindness towards them. Ask them to share the experience and then share their feelings towards the person who gave the service. Encourage the entire class to perform a small act of kindness towards someone in the next two days. In two days, meet together again and allow everyone to share their experience and their feelings towards the person they performed the service for. Hopefully, everyone will recognize that whether you are the giver or the receiver, feelings of love increase for both people when acts of service are performed. Our feelings of love grow towards a person when we serve, as well as when we are served. Service is the "Magic Ingredient."

Day 115
Gentlemen Never Leave a Lady

A true gentleman is someone who always considers the heart and mind of a lady. With this in mind, it is good to assume that ladies (girls) are not always comfortable if left alone in certain situations. For instance, if you and your female friend are dropped off at a bus stop, it would be polite for you to walk her home or wait with her for her "ride" to come. This does not mean that you are "in love" with this lady. It simply is an act of courtesy and can contribute to her safety, as well. Likewise, if you and your friends go to a movie, and, upon your leaving the movie, everyone's parents are supposed to pick them up, it would be polite for at least one male to remain until all the females have been picked up. Gentlemen should never leave a lady alone on a sidewalk, at a bus stop, in a building, or in any other area where the lady could feel unsafe or uneasy. What is the definition of proper etiquette? You should know this by now: to help make others feel comfortable and valued. Consider this as you continue to refine (improve) your etiquette skills. See you next time.

Activity
It is important for males to start understanding their polite roles as a protector, comforter and example of admirable character. Hold on, this doesn't mean that women can't take care of themselves. We're talking manners here. We're helping young men to start recognizing that to be respectful, thoughtful, and courteous towards women is a sign of strength and integrity. To be a "gentleman," is an honor with a long tradition. The "pay offs" are huge, but sometimes, "time will have to tell."

Day 116
Borrowing Money

I wish that I could tell you to never borrow money from anyone; that would be the safest thing. However, life is full of surprises, and sometimes unavoidable events place us in situations that we would rather not be in, but we are. One of these situations is when we need to borrow money. Borrowing money from others is a delicate business and if it is not handled with extreme caution, it can lead to broken relationships and hurt feelings. Here are some guidelines that I hope you will consider if you ever need to borrow money, especially from your friends or family:

- **Before taking any money, both parties should agree upon the repayment schedule and terms (how, when, amount and any other details involving repayment) of the loan.**
- **Money should be paid back on time and according to the previous agreement.**
- **A gentleman should never borrow money from a lady.**
- **Be honest about your circumstances.**
- **KEEP YOUR WORD.**

I have witnessed family relationships torn apart because money was borrowed and never repaid. Please be cautious, and make sure you can keep the terms of an agreement regarding borrowing money. Our relationships in life are our greatest treasures. See you next time.

Activity
Now is a great time to have an economic lesson on borrowing money. What are appropriate reasons to borrow money and what are not? What is interest? How is interest accrued? Review and let your children see your loan agreements on your home and cars. Allow them to understand the actual amount you pay versus the payment without interest. Review credit cards and how using them carelessly can get us into big trouble. Many banks will send a representative to a class to help teach these principles and ideas. This could be an enrichment activity that takes an entire week.

Day 117
Sitting Gracefully

Knowing how to sit gracefully, regardless of whether we are male or female, is an important etiquette consideration to ensure that we do not send mixed messages or impolite suggestions. When we sit, we should always consider the audience we're sitting with. For instance, if we're sitting in school listening to our teacher lecture, it would not be appropriate to be "lounging" in our chair as if we're about to slide right out of it. This would send a message of extreme boredom, which would be rude to our teacher. Likewise, if we are sitting around the family room with our family or close friends, and we're sitting with our arms folded, our backs straight and our legs crossed, it might appear that we are upset, angry, or indifferent to those around us. A safe way to always sit that appears respectful, yet not aloof (uninterested), is to sit with our legs together, feet touching the ground, hands in our lap and back straight. This posture invites conversation, shows that we are interested in those around us, and yet gives a sense of deference (respect) as well. Try to be more aware of your posture, and realize that our posture can send messages to others. Also, it is a good idea to make sure that the clothes we wear are suitable for how and where we're sitting. For instance, if we have a dress on, it would probably not be appropriate to sit on the ground. Let's make sure that the way we sit is not only respectful to others but to ourselves as well. See you next time.

Do these people look interested in what they are learning or extremely bored?

Activity
Continue with this discussion and allow the children to practice sitting respectfully. Have fun letting the children sit different ways and then allow the other children to discuss what their body language suggests about how they feel. The goal of this exercise is to simply encourage the children to be more aware of how "body language" can send different messages, and to be more conscious of the messages they send.

Day 118
Unannounced Visits: a "No-No"

Have you ever heard a knock at the door and then you hear your mom scream from upstairs, "Don't you dare open that door!"? Well, besides the concern for safety, there are other reasons people sometimes don open the door. Their house may be a disaster. I'm sure that if there are kids in your home, you can relate to your house becoming disastrous and a bit frightening. This is why it is not polite to try to visit someone unannounced. We need to warn people that we're coming. Give them a chance to clean up a bit, both their homes and themselves, so that they feel better about themselves and the condition of their home. It is amazing what you can throw into the bathtub, dryer, or of course, closets, when you need to get rid of things quickly. I just hope no one ever tries to look behind my shower curtain when they come to visit. Also, we never know what is going on in someone's home. Maybe there's a birthday party going on, or a romantic dinner taking place. In such cases, the homeowners would prefer not to be interrupted. Many things can be going on which would prevent the homeowners from wanting to answer the door. Unannounced visits are a big "no-no," so don't get your feelings hurt if you show up on someone's doorstep unannounced, and the door doesn't open, even though you know they're home. See you next time.

Activity

It's a good idea to have a plan in place for when you have unexpected guests. Go ahead and make assignments for times when you have guests coming over on short notice. For instance, assign someone to wipe down the guest bathroom, assign someone to spray room freshener and light candles, assign someone to run the vacuum over the room where guests will be, etc. Keep a "homemade" frozen dinner in your freezer at all times. Let your children help plan what it will be, as well as help prepare it. If, after a month or two, there is no guest, go ahead and eat the dinner and then replace it with another meal in your freezer. These simple ideas really help and will allow you to enjoy unexpected guests instead of having a "panic attack."

Day 119
Judge Not

I know we all have heard at sometime in our life, "Don't judge others." Why is it rude to judge others? What do you think? When we judge someone, we form an opinion about them. Usually we do this by watching their behavior, and then we apply our own values to determine whether their behavior is right or wrong. What if someone doesn't share the same values that we do? What if someone sees five minutes of our behavior and then forms an opinion about what kind of person we are, and whether they want to be associated with us or not? Have you ever had five minutes, during which if someone had seen your behavior, they might not think very "highly" of you? Of course you have, because we all have. It's like taking a snapshot of your life and judging everything about you from one picture. Unless we have walked in someone else's shoes, lived in their home, shared the exact same experiences as they (which is impossible), we can never fairly judge anyone. Not accurately, at least. It's OK to not agree with someone's behavior, but be careful about forming opinions about people. We never know what kind of morning someone could have had, or whether someone is suffering from a loss or a sickness. In other words, we don't know exactly what is going on in most people's lives, so it's not polite to judge others, but to respect them as human beings and look for the good in everyone. See you next time.

Activity
This is a really important topic to discuss and usually is an easy one that kids enjoy and are interested in discussing. Begin the discussion by asking everyone if they have ever felt judged? What did it feel like? Did you think the judgment was fair? Why or why not? Next, ask if they have ever judged someone? This is a little tricky. We're not trying to embarrass anyone. It is important, however, for the children to recognize what judging is so that they know what to avoid. Use examples. For instance, you could ask, "Has anyone ever thought that someone was probably not real smart because of the way they were dressed?" "Have you ever not picked someone for your team, because they didn't look like they would be good at sports?" "Have you ever avoided someone because someone else told you they were weird or had strange beliefs?" "Have you ever assumed something about someone because of the color of their skin?" This discussion can take several turns, depending on how the children respond. Just allow the discussion to take shape and, hopefully, it will open everyone's eyes to the risks and unfairness of judging.

Day 120
Etiquette Regarding Other Customs and Beliefs

It is polite to be sensitive to other people's beliefs and customs. Educating ourselves on other religions and beliefs can help us to better understand one another. It's hard to communicate and befriend people if we don't understand why they do certain things, and why they react in certain ways. Learning about each other is a great first step in ensuring that we do not offend or misunderstand one another. We can do this as we listen. Listening is a great skill that allows us to learn. "If you're talking, you aint a learning," as my grandma used to say. When we honor others' beliefs, this doesn't mean we have to participate in their religious rituals or other customs; it simply means that we allow them to participate without criticism or judgment on our part. We don't make fun of or announce to them the "error of their ways". We respect their opinions and we acknowledge that they have every right to believe and feel the way they want to, as long as it does not hurt others. Isn't that what we want? Isn't that truly why America was founded? Yes, it was. Show respect to all people by honoring the beliefs of all people. See you next time.

Activity
This is a great time to educate your students on the basic beliefs and customs of the different principal faiths in our world: Christiananity, Judaism, Buddhism and Islam. Remember, the purpose of this assignment is to promote understanding, not criticism. It's important to look for ways in which these religions are alike, as well as different. If you have friends of these faiths, invite them to come and share with your class why their faith is important to them. There is a time and place to testify to others. I have found that before I can testify, I need to be trusted and have true friendships with others. Begin by building your understanding of others, and then see where it takes you.

Day 121
Funerals

realize that this might be uncomfortable for some or all of you to talk about. However, there are some important etiquette rules that we need to consider. Allow me to explain a few things to help us better understand and be more prepared for these occasions. What are "pallbearers"? Pallbearers are usually six or eight men who are close friends of the deceased, who are chosen by the family to help carry the casket. Close relatives should never be chosen as pallbearers, because their place during this time is with the women of the family. As a courtesy, friends usually record the names of people who have given food and flowers to the family during this time. This helps the family to be able to concentrate on more important matters. At the cemetery, it is impolite to walk on the graves. Do your best to avoid walking directly on the graves, although sometimes it may be unavoidable. Wearing dark clothes to a funeral service is a way of showing the family that you join them in their mourning for their loved one. We never want to wear anything to a funeral that would distract from the service or the family members. Children should only attend funerals if they can be reverent and obedient. It's difficult to talk about, but our behavior at a funeral can be a source of great strength to those who are mourning. See you next time.

Activity

I believe that the best way to start this discussion is to simply ask your students, "Do you have any questions about what happens at a funeral, or why?" Just allow the discussion to "take shape" according to the children's comments and questions. Usually we fear what we don't understand. It's a lot easier to discuss these things before we're faced with a loved one's departure. We are more open to ask questions without letting our emotions get the best of us. Be gentle with younger children, and focus on the customs and rituals of your faith and traditions. Discuss ways that your students can show their concern for friends and family who suffer these losses.

Day 122
Biking Etiquette

Biking etiquette not only helps with our manners, it increases our safety, as well. Here is a list of some biking considerations that serve two purposes: manners and safety. Review the list and discuss it with your class.

1. Stay to the right. Bikers should follow the same driving pattern as a car, which means staying on the right side of a road, trail, or sidewalk.
2. Bikers should bike in a single file when biking around traffic or people.
3. Bikers should obey all traffic laws, such as stopping at red lights and stop signs, giving proper signaling when turning and observing "pedestrian right of way".
4. Bikers should wear brightly colored clothes during the day and reflective wear when it becomes dark, to ensure that others see them.
5. Bikers should always wear a helmet.
6. Bikers should keep a safe distance between each other, so that there is less chance of running into each other.
7. Bikers should ride in straight lines, avoiding "zigzagging", so that people can predict their behavior.
8. Bikers should have a horn or bell on their bike to warn others of their upcoming approach.

Enjoy your next biking trip, and use your biking etiquette to make sure that everyone else enjoys the trip, as well. See you next time.

Activity
Well, this is an easy activity. Plan a biking trip to some place you haven't explored yet (the Virginia Creeper is awesome) and then GO! Make sure that all your students are clear on biking etiquette, and then go and enjoy a lovely day on a bike trail.

Day 123
Wedding Etiquette

Weddings and wedding receptions are such special occasions. There are a host of etiquette considerations surrounding wedding behavior, both for the host and the guest; however we are only going to "touch" on a few concerning the guest. When we receive a wedding invitation, the invitation will have specific names on the invitation, stating exactly who is invited. If the invitation says, "The McKellar Family", then, obviously, the entire family is invited. However, if the invitation only reads, "Mr. and Mrs. McKellar," then they are the only ones invited. It is rude to call and ask if you can bring more guests than those included on the invitation. This etiquette consideration is true for all invitations, whether for a party, a dinner, a wedding, or other occasion. If you've been invited to a wedding and cannot attend, it is polite to nevertheless, send a gift. When attending a wedding or wedding reception, it is not polite to wear all white. The bride is usually dressed all in white, and we want her to feel special and "stand out" from the crowd. It is her day to "shine." We don't want to wear anything that would draw attention away from the bride and groom. It is not appropriate to wear hats to a wedding. In general, our overall behavior should be respectful and joyful for the bride and groom. Remember, this is their day, so making sure that all the attention is on them is a great way to honor their celebration. See you next time.

Activity
This is simply for fun and for dreaming.

For Girls: Get a poster, bridal magazines, home décor magazines, travel magazines and some arts and crafts supplies. Allow the girls to decorate their "wedding poster" with their name, decorations and "wish" pictures of their wedding dress, wedding location, wedding cake, engagement ring, honeymoon location, and future house. They will love this!

For Boys: Get a poster, car magazines, home magazines, college locations, etc., and allow the boys to make their "future poster"; which will include: their name, "wish" pictures of their future car, college, job description, house, "toys," and any other "wish" list. Basically, this allows the children to visualize their future and, remind them that these things take a lot of education, dedication and persistence to achieve.

Day 124
Exiting & Entering An Elevator

When we are waiting to enter an elevator, it is polite to allow everyone to exit the elevator before we try to get on. Make sure to stand to the side of the elevator while we're waiting, so that we are not "in the way" when people are trying to exit. Once everyone is off, then you may enter. When exiting the elevator, always allow women and the elderly to exit before anyone else. If no one seems to move, simply say, "Please, after you." As people are exiting, hold the door open with your hand, or press the "door open" button until everyone is off. While riding on the elevator, try not to speak too loudly, talk on your cell phone, release any "bodily functions," or do anything that would make others feel uncomfortable in such "close quarters." See you next time.

Day 125
Practice at Home

As you have learned, there are many etiquette skills and considerations. I hope that you have enjoyed learning about them, but more importantly, I hope that you have enjoyed practicing them and working them into your lives. One thing I know: we can't be one person at home and then try to be another person in public. Our true self always shines through. This is why it is so important that we practice these principles in our homes, so that when we go out in public, these polite considerations will come easily and naturally. Mom and Dad must be the example. Children, of course, do what they see more often than what they hear. If children see uncontrolled temper, hear gossip, witness unkindness, observe arrogance or sharp dealings with others, their own character will surely suffer. Be the person that you want your children to become. Children, be the person that you know you can be. As always, enjoy one another; enjoy helping others to feel more valued and at ease. As we do, our own self worth and self respect will increase and our happiness will grow. So what is self respect? You tell me. Hope to meet you someday.

Completion Checklist

Once the child has read the daily lesson, and explained it to one (or both) of their parents, then have one parent or guardian sign, date, and check the box as completed.

Lesson #	Check	Signature	Date	Lesson #	Check	Signature	Date
1	✓			41			
2	✓			42			
3	✓			43			
4	✓			44			
5	✓			45			
6	✓			46			
7	✓			47			
8	✓			48			
9	✓			49			
10	✓			50			
11	✓			51			
12	✓			52			
13	✓			53			
14	✓			54			
15	✓			55			
16	✓			56			
17	✓			57			
18	✓			58			
19	✓			59			
20	✓			60			
21	✓			61			
22	✓			62			
23	✓			63			
24	✓			64			
25				65			
26				66			
27				67			
28				68			
29				69			
30				70			
31				71			
32				72			
33				73			
34				74			
35				75			
36				76			
37				77			
38				78			
39				79			
40				80			

Lesson #	Check	Signature	Date	Lesson #	Check	Signature	Date
81				104			
82				105			127
83				106			
84				107			
85				108			
86				109			
87				110			
88				111			
89				112			
90				113			
91				114			
92				115			
93				116			
94				117			
95				118			
96				119			
97				120			
98				121			
99				122			
100				123			
101				124			
102				125			
103							